DEVOTIONAL COMMENTARY

THE
Blessing

uniting generations

Brian & Candice Simmons

BroadStreet
PUBLISHING

BroadStreet Publishing® Group, LLC
Savage, Minnesota, USA
BroadStreetPublishing.com

The Blessing: *Uniting Generations*

Stock or custom editions of BroadStreet Publishing titles may be purchased in bulk for educational, business, ministry, fundraising, or sales promotional use. For information, please email orders@broadstreetpublishing.com.

Cover and interior by Garborg Design at GarborgDesign.com

Printed in the United States of America

20 21 22 23 24 5 4 3 2 1

I will pour refreshing water on the thirsty
and streams on the dry ground.
I will pour out my Spirit on your children,
my blessing upon your descendants.
They will spring up like grass blanketing a meadow,
like poplars growing by gushing streams.

ISAIAH 44:3–4

CONTENTS

FOREWORD

Imagine *The Blessing* in your hands as a prophetic compass from heaven. It contains secrets that the Father is whispering.

Years ago, I had a vision. I saw a map of the world. As I was looking closely, I noticed oak trees. Some regions and cities had giant oak trees while some had smaller ones. Then the scene changed. I saw trees dying, except in the regions where the smaller trees grew up right next to the giant oak trees. God spoke to me and said, "This will be the blessing of the generations. Where you see young and old together, the kingdom will flourish. Where you see isolation and rebellion, it will be hindered."

I have known Dr. Brian and Candice Simmons for over seventeen years. The majority of that time they have been my spiritual parents. Pastor Brian and Candice, Pop and Mom as we call them, have been the driving force behind all the churches we have started and the move of God we have seen in New England. Years ago God orchestrated our relationship, and through every season we have stayed submitted and committed to one another. Some of the greatest truths they live by are poured into this book.

From their faithfulness to being missionaries in the jungle of Panama, to building a mega church in Connecticut, to now travelling the world with the Passion Translation, I have often wondered how a generation could tap into the blessing and breakthrough on their lives. Considering how extremely busy they are, I realize not everyone has the privilege my wife and I have learning directly from them. I believe fully that this book is the answer. These pages display the heart and impartation from the authors. It's a "follow me as I have followed Christ" anointing. This blessing taught about in these pages is the believer's blessing; it's your birthright from the Lord.

The apostle Paul said in 2 Timothy 1:5: "I'm filled with joy as I think of your strong faith that was passed down through your family line. It began with your grandmother Lois, who passed it on to your dear mother, Eunice. And it's clear that you too are following in the footsteps of their godly example." God's desire is that you receive a blessing of inheritance today. I did not grow up in a family with any heritage in faith. However, through the very teachings explained in *The Blessing*, I have received from the Lord as if I have been in a family of faith for many generations.

Get ready to step into another dimension of blessing, a realm in God where generational curses are broken, family lines are healed, and the DNA of heaven is flooding your family, home, workplace, and city.

Get ready to have your faith ignited as you embark on a journey into the miraculous.

Get ready to receive the Father's plan for your life.

Let these pages be an invitation into the greater glory realm.

As I read this book, I could hear the Father whisper, "Come up higher." Here we come, Lord!

James B. Levesque, D.D.

INTRODUCTION

Abraham, Isaac, and Jacob. What amazing men they were, and what amazing heroes of faith are their descendants. Their lives are rich examples of how God transforms our hearts today. Every believer in Jesus Christ has a blessing given to us in Christ through the promises God gave to these three men.

For Abraham, it was the faith-promise of children, land, and blessing. Abraham is truly the father of our faith. He opened the faith-door that accessed heaven's blessings and favor. Leaving everything behind, he stepped out into a faith-journey that led him to his inheritance. Tested over and over, he was found faithful. We need the faith of Abraham that builds altars of testimony with our every breakthrough.

For Isaac, it was his sonship that brought the blessing. He was the son of promise, the son of supernatural power. Everything about Isaac's story points us to the faith-inheritance that comes to us simply by being a son or a daughter. Isaac re-dug ancient wells and opened up new ones. Sons of inheritance will drink from the wells of the past but will always dig new ones. We need the sonship of Isaac to understand our inheritance and dig new wells of glory.

For Jacob, it was his transformation from being a "heel-grabber" to become a "prince with God." Everything about the story of Jacob points us to the power of God to transform us into a royal partner with heaven. Jacob stole the birthright from Esau, pulled the wool over Isaac's eyes, and ended up wrestling with the Midnight Man. But at last, we see the transformation of a man who became the father of twelve princes—the twelve tribes of Israel. We need the transformation of Jacob to become our life story.

Our God is the God of Abraham, Isaac, and Jacob. That means we can expect the inheritance of God's covenant to flow through the generations until we are transformed. What these three patriarchs went through is a picture of what God is going to do in every royal believer today (1 Corinthians 10:11). The dealings of God with Abraham, Isaac, and Jacob typify the foundation of all that God plans to do in the human soul. Abraham discovered Yahweh as the God of promise. Isaac found him to be the God of miracles. And Jacob learned that he is the God of transformation. Each patriarch received the promise of miracles, and this miracle-promise released true transformation within the heart of each man.

God has a blessing of inheritance for all of us as well.[1] And we can experience it in our lives today. We too often put off until tomorrow the things that are available to us today in Christ. As we begin to see the Father as the patriarchs began to see him, we, too, can experience true fellowship with the One our heart loves. He has done all the preparatory work for us. He has purchased it all for us by the blood of his cross. With his divine perspective in our hearts, we can step into our inheritance right here on earth. Do you want to see what he sees? In the midst of turmoil, you can look at all of life through his heavenly perspective. God the Father never saw Abram as a man with a wife who was too old to birth a child. He saw Sarah's barrenness as a way to display his glory to all people by doing the impossible. When we think that it's too late, he sees opportunity.

We see in Abraham, Isaac, and Jacob that God longed for more than just a man. He longed for more than one nation or peoples. He longed to see every nation, tribe, and tongue drawn to him. He loved Jesus so much that he wanted to fill heaven with people just like him. This was his reason for calling Abram out of the land of Ur and bringing him to himself.

It's time for you to choose this God to be your very own inheritance. It is the desperate walk of the hungry to move out of our own reality and into his. You are called to be his, now and forever, a look-alike of Jesus. Though made from dust, we are destined for glory. This is our divine inheritance that unites us all. This is the inheritance passed down to us from God, the God of Abraham, the God of Isaac, and the God of Jacob. He is the God who gives inheritances that unite generations.

Abraham is the ancestor of Jesus Christ, and from him has come a people who know their God. A people who know their destiny. A people who walk in unity and in love. From the first Adam to the last Adam, the story will be complete as the church "aris[es] as the dayspring of the dawn, fair as the shining moon. Bright and brilliant as the sun in all its strength. Astonishing to behold" (Song of Songs 6:10). Yes, one day there will be a people on this earth who will display the image of their Father God. And so, we start this book where our first book, *The Image Maker*, left off. We must have an understanding of the first family of the nations for us to understand God's purposes on the earth. The days of your spiritual inheritance are before you now.

LET'S PRAY

Father, today, I step out by faith into this adventure with you. I want to know you and to understand your ways. Reveal your power to me. Increase my faith. Enlarge my joy. Transform my soul. I want to appropriate and enjoy the fullness of my inheritance in Christ. As I read this book, connect my heart to you as never before. I trust you completely! Amen.

1

Leave Everything Behind

The God of glory appeared to our ancestor Abraham.

Acts 7:2

The Bible is a book filled with the blessings of divine encounters. God walked with Adam and Eve, he spoke to Noah, he was more than a friend to Enoch, and he appeared as the Glory-God to Abram. Without divine encounters, we would not even have our Bible today.

The importance of the man Abram (who will later have his name changed to Abraham) is impossible to exaggerate. In fact, the story and lineage of Jesus begins with Abraham (Matthew 1:1–2). It was from Abraham that the nations were born!

Abraham had no burning bush to inspire him, no tablets of stone to guide him, and no ark of the covenant as a centerpiece of worship. Neither did Abraham have a temple to go to, a Bible to read, or a priest to counsel him. Nor did Abram have a pastor to pray for him, a prophet to prophesy to him, a teacher to instruct him, or a multitude of followers to validate him. But Abram had what God had always intended for those made in his image: he heard the voice of God.

ABRAM'S PARTIAL OBEDIENCE

> Terah took his son Abram, his grandson Lot, the son of Haran, and his daughter-in-law Sarai, his son Abram's wife, and they all departed together from the Chaldean city of Ur to go into the land of Canaan. But when they journeyed as far as Haran, they settled there. (Genesis 11:31)

God spoke to Abram when he was almost fifty years old and told him to leave his country, his people, and his father's household and to go to a land God would reveal to him (Acts 7:1–3). Instead, we see Abram gathering up his father and his father's entire household and moving them all with him to a place called Haran. It was while they were in Haran that Abram's father, Terah, died. Only after Terah died did Abram leave and complete the journey.

Abram was slow to fully obey the word of the Lord. He compromised by taking all his clan with him. He stopped short of where he was called to go, and he disobeyed by taking his support system along with him. By failing to leave *all* behind, Abram found himself in a spiritual pause at Haran.

The name *Terah* means "lagging behind" or "delay." There was a delay in God's plan for Abram because he took his father with him. This delay ended up being twenty-five years. We, too, can delay God's plan for our lives when we fail to fully obey. There was a time in our lives (Brian and Candice) when God spoke to us about leaving the mission field and returning to North America. Yet it took us nearly two years to fully obey what God had instructed us to do. That delay was a season of difficulty, burnout, and disorientation—until we obeyed the voice of the Lord. We know from firsthand knowledge that every self-imposed delay in our lives must be forsaken. There is only one call on our lives—a call to obedience, no matter what the cost! When we obeyed and returned to our home nation, the favor on our lives returned and has increased until this day. Praise God!

How often we lag behind in reaching the place of promise by taking with us what we should have left behind. The ties of human nature hindered the full response of Abram's heart. Terah is a picture of our old self (the old man) that must die before we can enter in to our inheritance. Compromises will lead to delays in the unfolding of God's destiny for us.

Abram had a "Lot" to lose. Although Terah was gone, Abram still had his nephew, Lot, who accompanied him, and many sorrows in their relationship would later surface. Abram set out for the land of his inheritance, but once again, he settled far short of where God wanted to bring him. Eventually, Abram was forced to leave all his family, including Lot, to fulfill the full plan of God for his life.

It has been the purpose of the author of Genesis to bring us to this point. Everything from Genesis 1–11 has been introductory in nature. Incredibly informative and amazingly accurate but only anticipating what is about to come. God the Father places a "spiritual seed" in the heart of Abram. Chosen by the God of heaven, the story line now takes us into God's ultimate purposes.

All of Abraham's life is meant to bring us into an understanding of our own heavenly calling, to a blessing beyond description.

When we begin to have an understanding of our inheritance, we will find the cure for the disease of seeking the satisfaction of making a name for ourselves here on earth. How could we love the things of the world when we have been given "every spiritual blessing in the heavenly realm" in Christ? We have only to match our condition with our position. Why would we delay or compromise when we understand what is ours already? We must continue reaching into the place God has destined for us. Halfway is not enough.

Like Abram, we are called to a life of separation. But, as we all know, we delay in answering that call at times because a near relative is not prepared for a life outside the box. It took death for Abram to break that tie to the world, and so it took death for us; it's called the cross of Christ, the place where we were co-crucified with him, the place of separation from the world, along with our co-burial and co-resurrection with him to release us to the purposes of God. The same cross that connects us to God separates us from the world (Galatians 6:14). Our "Terah" has died, and now we must move forward in the resurrection power imputed to us and move forward toward the destiny that God has already secured for us.

When you read about Abram in the New Testament, you will find that God graciously overlooks this failure of Abram. "Faith motivated Abraham to obey God's call and leave the familiar to discover the territory he was destined to inherit from God. So he left with only a promise and without even knowing ahead of time where he was going, Abraham stepped out in faith" (Hebrews 11:8). Grace had blotted out his sin.

OUR SPIRITUAL CALLING

Try to imagine what that must have seemed for Abram to leave everything behind and go somewhere. I can imagine him saying, *Where are we going, Lord?* The essence of what the Lord said to Abram sounded something like this:

> "Leave it all behind—your native land, your people, your relatives, all your stuff, your security, your dreams— release them all to come with me. I'm sending you somewhere you've never been before. You're going to do something that no one has ever done before. Step out into the unknown and I will go with you. Concerning the destination: I'll let you know when we get there! Your part is only to go; my part is to know. Follow me, and I will make you into a great nation. I will bless your socks off and prosper you beyond your imagination. I will make you so famous that everyone will know about your journey. You will be a tremendous source of blessing for others. Your blessing will rub off on everyone who blesses you. And if anyone tries to stop you, I will stop them! And through you, believe it or not, the entire earth will be blessed. Now let's get going!" (Genesis 12:1–3, author's paraphrase)

After being visited by the Lord, Abram had a choice to make. He could allow the voice of God to move him in a totally new direction, or he could stay where he was. Abram would be lost and disappointed forever if he did not obey this God who appeared to him. God must be everything to this man of faith. The promise of inheritance gripped his heart. It would be greater than what he already possessed, something bigger than himself.

The essence of our "spiritual calling" is the same as Abram's. We love Jesus beyond any other affection. Lovers of Jesus will leave everything behind to follow his calling, his footsteps, even when it doesn't make sense. Faith moves us closer to our inheritance until, finally, we discover the fullness God created us for.

LET'S PRAY

Father, today, I ask for your fire to fill my heart and consume everything in me that lags behind and delays to obey your voice. I want to be a true follower of Jesus and a person of great faith. Show me today how I can love you and serve you even more completely. This world has nothing for me. I find all my joys and all my fountains in you. Amen.

2

SEVEN TESTS OF ABRAHAM

Now Yahweh said to Abram: "Leave it all behind—your native land,[2] your people, your father's household, and go to the land that I will show you. Follow me, and I will make you into a great nation. I will exceedingly bless and prosper you, and I will make you famous,[3] so that you will be a tremendous source of blessing for others. I will bless all who bless you and curse all who curse you. And through you all the families of the earth will be blessed."[4] So Abram obeyed Yahweh and left; and Lot went with him.

GENESIS 12:1–4

Has God ever told you to do something difficult, painful, or impossible? Imagine how you would feel if these words were spoken to you? Wouldn't it seem like God is asking a lot from his servant? Yet if God instructs you to do something for him, you can count on his promise of power to fulfill it. God's promise to Abram guarded his heart and energized his steps. He had the truest form of security that exists in this universe: walking in the clear direction of the Lord.

Abraham's life is a story of separations that he had to make. Each new separation brought new revelation. Each new revelation led to greater worship. Abraham would make a separation, and then the Lord would speak to him. And each time it prompted him to make an altar of worship. Here are the seven separations of Abraham's life. Each of them was a test of his faith. And each represents a parallel test for us in our own journey. To follow Christ means you leave everything behind. The world behind me, Jesus before me. Here are the seven things that Abram (Abraham) had to leave behind:

1. He had to leave his *comfort zone* (Genesis 12:1). He had to forsake all that was familiar and comfortable. He had to abandon the land governed by moon-worship (the powers of darkness). He had to leave his home country and journey into a promised land of destiny's fulfillment. We, too, must leave the traditions that say, "You can go so far but no farther." We may need to discard traditions and boundaries. God wants you to leave the familiar, get out of your comfort zone, and go into the glory zone. Philippians 3:14 states, "I run straight for the divine invitation of reaching the heavenly goal and gaining the victory-prize through the anointing of Jesus."

2. He had to leave his *closest ties*, his father's household (Genesis 12:1). God's call of faith on our lives will one day deal with the closest ties of our heart. This represents both our natural and spiritual kindred. Often

19

our sincere (but mistaken) family members will urge us not to leave our current condition and beckon us to stay behind with them. Many within the church will refuse to let you go into the place of your inheritance, seeking to keep you in their system. According to Job 17:9, "The righteous keep moving forward" (NLT).

3. Abraham had to leave Egypt and his *compromise* with the world (Genesis 13:1). Egypt was only a stopping place, not his destination. Egypt is a type of world-system full of the lusts of the flesh, the lusts of the eyes, and the pride of life. It's a place of bondage to the man-pleasing spirit that seeks prominence over others. Doubting God's provision in a famine is what drove him to this compromise. It's the land of lies and deception. To refuse to leave Egypt is to continue in bondage and servitude.

"Don't continue to team up with unbelievers in mismatched alliances, for what partnership is there between righteousness and rebellion? Who could mingle light with darkness? What harmony can there be between Christ and Satan? Or what does a believer have in common with an unbeliever? What friendship does God's temple have with demons? For indeed, we are the temple of the living God, just as God has said: 'I will make my home in them and walk among them…I will be a true Father to you, and you will be my beloved sons and daughters,' says the Lord Yahweh Almighty." (2 Corinthians 6:14–18)

4. Abram had to separate from *wrong companions*. He eventually left Lot behind (Genesis 13:11). Lot was not a man of the Spirit but of the flesh. He lived only from a carnal and worldly viewpoint. (I am not suggesting that you abandon family completely, but there is a spiritual principle that we don't continue a close relationship with those who hinder our forward advance with God.) "Stop fooling yourselves! Evil companions will corrupt good morals and character" (1 Corinthians 15:33). Some people are just along for the ride but despise the responsibilities. The friends you keep can define and describe you. Choose your friends wisely, ones that will help you grow in character.

5. Abram had to forsake his *craving for wealth*. He refused the spoils of Sodom (Genesis 14:21–24). After rescuing his nephew Lot and returning all the stolen goods to the king of Sodom, he gave it all back. He even paid tithes to the priest of Salem (Jerusalem), Melchizedek. "And Melchizedek, who was both a priest of the Most High God and the king of Salem, brought out to Abram bread and wine. He spoke over him a special blessing, saying, 'Blessed is Abram by God Most High, Creator of heaven and earth. And blessed be God Most High. Whose power delivered your enemies into your hands!' Abram gave Melchizedek a tenth of all he possessed. Then the king of Sodom said to Abram, 'Just give me the people you rescued; keep all the spoils for yourself.' But Abram said to the king of Sodom, 'I raised my

hand to Yahweh, God Most High, and I pledged a solemn oath to the Possessor of heaven and earth that I would keep nothing for myself that belongs to you, not even a thread of a garment or sandal strap. That way, you will never be able to say, "I was the one that made Abram rich"" (vv. 18–23). Great privilege and anointing will provide opportunity to get wealth. God will provide unlimited provision to those who seek first the kingdom of God. The man of faith must not be bought. First Samuel 2:7 tells us, "The Lord sends poverty and wealth; he humbles and he exalts" (NIV).

6. Abraham had to leave behind his *clever ideas* and the works of the flesh. He had to separate himself from Ishmael (Genesis 21:9–14). Ishmael was the product of his impatience, not the child of promise. Every manufactured attempt to forward the promise of God must be abandoned. Ishmael was Abraham's good idea, but not God's promise. "As you yield freely and fully to the dynamic life and power of the Holy Spirit, you will abandon the cravings of your self-life.... Keep in mind that we who belong to Jesus, the Anointed One, have already experienced crucifixion. For everything connected with our self-life was put to death on the cross and crucified with Messiah. We must live in the Holy Spirit and follow after him" (Galatians 5:16, 24–25).

7. Abraham gave up and let go of his *dearest treasure*, his beloved son, the son of prophetic promise, Isaac

(Genesis 22:1–14). This was his ultimate test of friendship with God. He had to give up even the promise God had fulfilled. And we find in Hebrews the reason Abraham could do what he did. Because he believed the second part of the promise that the Lord had given him. Hebrews 11:17–19 says, "Faith operated powerfully in Abraham for when he was put to the test he offered up Isaac. Even though he received God's promises of descendants, he was willing to offer up his only son! For God had promised, 'Through your son Isaac your lineage will carry on your name.' Abraham's faith made it logical to him that God could raise Isaac from the dead, and symbolically, that's exactly what happened."

Of course, God does not call us to sacrifice or abandon our children, but rather, it's a hyperbole to help us understand how intent we must be to not worship or hold the long-awaited promises we have received as more important than the worship of our Lord God and Father. Our long-awaited promises, the ones for which we have fought the good fight of faith and won, cannot be our focus of worship. For our worship must be reserved for God and God alone. Exodus 20:3 states, "You shall have no other gods before me" (NIV).

And this also speaks to our trust in God. Do we believe his words, the report of the Lord? And do we believe that his character is good? Abraham knew logically that if the Lord asked him to sacrifice his own son, then he would have to raise him up again. Otherwise, how could he trust in a God who doesn't keep his promises? All the promises of God are yes and amen!

LET'S PRAY

My wonderful Father in heaven, you always know what is best for me. When I feel like I'm surrounded by impossibilities, I'm actually surrounded by you. Every command you speak to me is a promise. Your words are promises that I will succeed and reach the prize of the goal of being like Christ. I trust your words, even the words I don't understand. I know that you hold the timing of my life in your hands. I rest in you. Amen.

3

OBEY THE VOICE OF GOD

"Leave...your native land...
Go to the land that I will show you."
GENESIS 12:1

Before we turn to discuss Abraham's seven promises of blessing, let's take a look at the setting. As the men of Babel sought to
build for themselves an earthly city, Abraham proved his willing-
ness to abandon all in search of a heavenly city. Abraham's entire
life is a story of leaving all to follow the Lord. Much like Peter, who
left his nets and boats and fishing business, Abram left his country,
his family. He continually released everything to God. The gospel
of Jesus Christ truly begins with a man named Abram who listened
and obeyed God (Matthew 1:1). All of human history has been
changed because Abram heard and followed a heavenly vision.

And you are an heir of the blessing God promised Abraham,

for you and I are the true spiritual seed. All the blessings given to him now flow to you. God will bless whatever you touch, for the blessing of Abraham is upon you. Your life is anointed to prosper, to grow, to excel, to bless others, to increase, and to be a source of blessing to your family, your church, your city. Nothing can stop you as you step out in faith![5]

In a way that Abram could never forget, "the God of glory" first appeared to Abram while in Ur, a city in ancient Iraq (Acts 7:2). Think of that—the God of glory manifested in front of Abram! The celestial vision resulted in a call to Abram that shaped his destiny. He probably never dreamed that God would call him. Many people today have no clue that God has called them to greatness. This "appearing" was so life changing for Abram that it enabled him to come out of his pagan, darkened background and accept God's calling on his life. The glory of another world drew Abram out of the city of Ur and to the city of God.

This is the first time God "appeared" since he walked with Adam and Eve in the cool of the day. We don't read that he appeared to Abel or Noah but to Abram. As a man would speak face-to-face with his friend, God appears. He saw the God of glory! It was perhaps this vision that kept Abram moving through his tent-dwelling days. Abram was able to believe God because he was a man of spiritual vision. This visitation made Abram's future as real as the present.

Isaac could be offered as a sacrifice because Abram could see ahead to the ultimate sacrifice of Jesus and even the power for resurrection (John 8:56). Abram, the prophet, had foreseen the crucifixion and resurrection of Jesus prophetically and knew that his son would be a picture of the coming Messiah. Abram was a man captured with the eternal.

Abram was not told to stay and reform the culture or run for political office. He was called to separate himself and go out of Ur/Iraq toward another city. He didn't know where he was going, but he did know what he was looking for (Hebrews 11:8–10). He was told to leave his country, his kindred, his father's house, and leave for a country that God would lead him to: "Go to the land that I will show you."

Led by revelation, Abraham was to live a life of obedience, simply following each moment with the leading of God. And so, we also are to live that kind of life. If we listen to his voice and his Word, we will step into the new thing God is doing today. His guidance is unmistakable when we fix our hearts on him. He can lead us to our spouse, to the right church, where to pursue our education, and the career or ministry he has in store for us. He will lead us in our calling. As we lean our hearts into him, he leads us and directs us by the Holy Spirit.

It was by faith that Abraham obeyed when God called him to leave home. And it was by faith that he moved to another land that God would give him as his inheritance. He was willing to go without knowing where he was going. And even when he reached the land God promised him, he had to live by faith. For he was like a foreigner, living in tents. And so did Isaac and Jacob, who inherited the same promise. Abraham was confidently looking forward for a city with eternal foundations, a city designed and built by God.

For years I have focused on the unique faith Abraham possessed that helped him leave a secure life to engage a new life without a known destination. "He left with only a promise and without even knowing ahead of time where he was going" (v. 8).

These words are so powerful that they almost overshadow what comes in the next verse.

In verses nine through ten, the writer of Hebrews says, "He lived by faith as an immigrant in his promised land as though it belonged to someone else. He journeyed through the land living in tents with Isaac and Jacob who were persuaded that they were also co-heirs of the same promise. His eyes of faith were set on the city with unshakable foundations, whose architect and builder is God himself." He continued to live in tents like he was only passing through. Abraham, our father of faith, is described as a man who finally made it to the land of promise, yet he continued to live like a foreigner in a tent. He remained mobile because he realized that something more was out ahead of him.

Like Abraham, we may need to be willing to leave some things behind. What are you allowing to determine your future? When we wait for all things to be known and predictable, we allow this to define how we live in the future. This life is only a temporary encampment—not a final destination. Abraham lived as a foreigner in a physical tent because God wanted him to remain mobile. We carry physical tents, bodies inhabited by the very presence of God that must remain open and available to his voice.

The key to moving forward is found in hearing and obeying the voice of God. Once you make this shift in your mindset, you'll find yourself moving forward into a new season of spiritual mobility. And the place will not be the determining factor when it comes to continuing to live in familiar surroundings or moving to another place. The difference will be your mindset and your response to what you hear.

Abraham lived in a tent in the land of promise. And this defined him as a foreigner because he was fixing his eyes on the fullness of a kingdom yet to be seen. His gaze of faith was foreign to those around him. He was looking at something they could not see. If we choose to live a life of faith, it may be a threat to others.

We may draw looks of suspicion from those around us who have chosen to settle and don't have eyes to see a new and emerging future. Settlers can end up protecting what they possess at the expense of future expanse. Foreigners, living in tents, by the very nature of their existence, make the status quo nervous because what a settled life has to offer is no longer appealing to the tent dweller. "For we have no city here on earth to be our permanent home, but we seek the city that is destined to come" (Hebrews 13:14).

Let's Pray

God, you are my strength. I can only move forward knowing that you are with me. To experience your presence and your grace is what keeps me moving. I love you, Father. Guide me, O Eternal God, into the place of perfect peace. Lead me on, King of Glory, until my resting place is in you. I want to go where you send me and be who you have called me to be. I love this journey into your heart. Go with me today. Amen.

4

God's Sevenfold Promise

"Follow me, and I will make you into a great nation. I will exceedingly bless and prosper you, and I will make you famous, so that you will be a tremendous source of blessing for others. I will bless all who bless you and curse all who curse you. And through you all the families of the earth will be blessed."

Genesis 12:2–3

Amazing! These prophetic promises to Abraham still live today, and Abraham's natural seed and his "spiritual seed," the church, fulfill them. If we are Christ's, then we are Abraham's seed and heirs according to these promises. There is a dual fulfillment embedded within these promises. Abraham received them through this divine encounter. We receive them through the divine encounter of the new birth.

We (Brian and Candice) feel blessed. We see it all around us.

No, we're not perfect, and our circumstances may not be perfect at any given moment, but we know that we are blessed. We read of God's blessing on the fish and birds. How much more will he bless his people! Each of us needs to know and feel the blessing of God that is over our lives.

The covenants of God are always to our benefit. They are "pacts of partnership" that are always tilted in our favor. The goodness of God is that he promises to bless us. God will never enter a covenant with his people and pull us into pain. He will pull us into pleasure. It is a covenant of redeeming grace and endless love that is the strength of God's faithfulness. Think about it— whenever God holds out his hand of covenant love to us, it is a win-win situation for us. We don't lose something good to gain something inferior. No, we lose all darkness and despair and gain the goodness of his promises. The God who made something out of nothing now gives to you and me something out of nothing.

God's loving heart is revealed as the One who delights in blessing his people. The idea of blessing is used in Genesis more than any other book: eighty-eight times compared to a total of 310 times in the rest of the Old Testament. God's plan is to bless the world—including you! God wants to see his covenant established in our lives, but that won't happen if we neglect it, are ignorant of it, or simply don't believe or understand it. So here's a quick over-view of the sevenfold promise to us through Abraham. Think of them as opportunities waiting for us to act upon.

THE SEVENFOLD PROMISE

1. "I WILL MAKE YOU INTO A GREAT NATION"

This new beginning for Abram would bring a blessing to a nation that was yet to be born. This is a prophecy of the nation of

Israel being formed from Abram's lineage. God's blessing would be upon this nation, and it would be great before God. Because he had left his nation, God would make Abraham into a *greater* nation. This is incredible. This would seem impossible, for Sarai had been barren her whole life. It would take a miracle to make a barren couple into a great nation. This would have greatly stretched his faith, yet he believed. God gave creative ability to Abraham, not only to produce offspring, but also to apply creative ability to form lasting enterprises that would shape a nation. God gave the ability to create community to Abram and his seed.

Not only did God give Abram the ability to birth a nation, but he also gave him the ability to create community and to form lasting enterprises that would shape that nation. To form lasting communities and shape a nation require great financial blessing, which was included in this covenant as well. This is a supernatural promise of a nation changing power through wealth strategies as well as multiplication in childbirth. And so today, this not only speaks of earthly wealth but also of the wealth of the gospel that transcends anything that money could buy. The blessing of Abraham has been passed down to us and has the ability to turn a lost and dying nation into a spiritual nation of greatness…so that we would broadcast his glorious wonders throughout the world (1 Peter 2:9). Out of one man came a nation of holy ones, recreated in his image.

2. "AND I WILL EXCEEDINGLY BLESS YOU AND PROSPER YOU"

This would more than make up for any loss of leaving his comfort zone. His greatest treasure was this blessing from God. The Father's blessing! Faith and Abram's obedience brought the blessing of God. Abram and God were to be friends. And implied in this blessing was fertility and offspring. This blessing would involve at least three promises: an heir, spiritual enjoyment, and material prosperity. He received them all. And they're ours as well! Who could curse the one God has blessed? A blessing has broken off the curse of sickness, poverty, and aborted dreams.

This covenant blessing implies great fruitfulness in our lives as we fellowship with the God of Abraham. And his super-abundance will be self-replicating, multiplying over and over. A stream of blessing that will continue and not diminish over time. This blessing comes from the promise of God that cannot be broken. The Father has come to bless you and to provide for you. It's time to walk by faith in the promise that says, "I *will* bless you!"

3. "I WILL MAKE YOU FAMOUS"

There is one name that is greater than all (Philippians 2:9–11; Revelation 15:4). How would God make Abram's name great? By exalting his name in the life of his servant. Every advance Abram made into greatness involved an altar where he offered more and more of himself to God. The Babel-builders sought to make a name for *themselves*, but here we find God saying to Abram that his name would be great: "I will make you famous."

So often we find opportunities to exalt ourselves, even in things of God. And just as the disciples of Jesus often competed over who would be the greatest, so we do the same today. God is not against fame. He's only against greatness that doesn't originate in him. Abram had much to go through before God could make his name famous on all the earth.

What does this mean to us as Abraham's spiritual offspring? It means that God will make our name famous as well. But mainly this speaks of having our vision enlarged to contain more than just one person, to contain a multitude. By changing Abram's name from "high and exalted father" to Abraham, meaning "father of a multitude," God greatly enlarged his vision from being one with an exalted name to being one with many sons of exaltation. This enlarged vision enabled Abraham to lead, create, birth enterprises, and walk into the future with confidence. So God has done the same with you! He has enlarged your faith-vision to move into the future so that others will share all that anointing of greatness that God has bestowed on you. Visionaries will shape the future. Those with the greatest vision win. This promise is the grace of empowerment of others (father of a multitude) given by the change of Abram's identity.

4. "YOU WILL BE A TREMENDOUS SOURCE OF BLESSING FOR OTHERS"

Abram's life from this day forward would bring untold blessing to others. Faith always blesses others. Abram could never have become Abraham if he had not left all to obey the call of God. He became a blessing to the nations because he walked in faith. And it's God's desire to make every true believer, like Abraham, a blessing to the nations. To be a blessing means to empower others in their spiritual lives, their wholeness, their relationships—every area of their lives. This, of course, includes and would not be complete without the empowerment to bless others with finances and wealth strategies. Abraham's seed is meant to bless others with wealth, through creating businesses, through extravagant generosity, and through wise strategies that will fund Christian enterprises around the world.

5. "I WILL BLESS ALL THOSE WHO BLESS YOU"

Those who endorsed and affirmed Abram would find enrichment and blessing from God. Those befriending him would receive blessing from the God of Glory. To honor the Jewish people is to honor the wisdom of God in choosing them to be a light to the nations. We bless God when we bless Israel. The blessing of Abraham will multiply to the church and to the individual that blesses the people of Abraham. Do you want to be financially and spiritually blessed? Then release a blessing to God's covenant people and watch it multiply back to you.

6. "I WILL CURSE ALL WHO CURSE YOU"

Anyone who treated Abram with contempt would be dishonored, cursed by God. So great was the blessing of Jehovah upon his life! Those who treated him with disrespect, God would remove blessing from them. This threat upon his enemies would be a source of strength to him all his days of pilgrimage. Just knowing this—knowing that any curse spoken over you will bring a curse on those who release it—will be a source of confidence to *you* as you move into your spiritual destiny. Let no one discourage you or turn you aside, child of Abraham!

7. "AND THROUGH YOU ALL THE FAMILIES OF THE EARTH WILL BE BLESSED"

Abram was to be a source of blessing to the whole world. No one would find divine blessing apart from Abram's seed. Salvation would come to the nations through the seed of Abraham, Jesus Christ our Lord (Matthew 1:1). God's blessing to Abram will only be fulfilled when it reaches to all the nations of the earth. This is the foundation of world missions. God's plan is not merely for a man or for a nation, but also for the whole world (John 3:16). Jesus Christ, our salvation, is the greatest blessing to this world (Acts 4:12).

You are a child of Abraham, filled with blessings, and given many wonderful promises. Galatians 3:8–9 states, "God's plan all along was to bring this message of salvation to the nations through the revelation of faith. Long ago God prophesied over Abraham, as the Holy Scriptures say: 'Through your example of faith all the nations will be blessed!' And so the blessing of Abraham's faith is now our blessing too!"

LET'S PRAY

Father God, you have blessed me with every spiritual blessing heaven contains. How could I ever comprehend all that you have done for me? My heart spills out with praise to you this day. Make my life a blessing to all whom I meet today. Make the words of my mouth a blessing to others. I want to make a difference in the world as I walk with you. I thank you for blessing me! Amen.

5

BUILD AN ALTAR
OF WORSHIP

So Abram obeyed Yahweh and left; and Lot went with him.
Now Abram was seventy-five years old when he departed from
Haran after his father died. He took his wife Sarai, his nephew Lot,
and all the possessions and people he had acquired in Haran; and
they departed for the land of Canaan. When they arrived in the
land of Canaan, Abram passed through the land and stopped at
the sacred site of Shechem, famous for the great oak tree of Moreh.
At that time, the Canaanites were also in the land.
Then Yahweh appeared before Abram and said, "This is the land
I will personally deliver to your seed." So Abram erected an altar
there to Yahweh, who had appeared before him. From there, he
journeyed on toward the hill country east of Bethel and pitched his
tent with Bethel on the west and Ai on the east. And there he built

another altar to Yahweh where he prayed and worshiped Yahweh.
Then Abram journeyed from there by stages through the southern
desert region.

GENESIS 12:4–9

ABRAM ARRIVES IN CANAAN

Abram was now seventy-five years old. His father had died, and the delay was over. He was told to leave all behind, but instead, he took Lot, his nephew, and others who had converted to the Yahweh. And later, Lot would prove to be a weight upon Abram's soul. For when we are called to leave it all and to go into the undiscovered country, whatever we choose to take with us will prove to be too heavy to bear.

So, they went out of Haran to go into the land of Canaan. With a fresh revelation in his heart, Abram and Sarai traveled till they arrived at Shechem[6] where they camped at the great tree of Moreh.[7] It was here that the Lord appeared to Abram again. Not only did Abram find the Canaanites in the land, but he also found the Lord. And God promised him that his offspring would inherit the land.

Each time God appeared to Abraham he built an altar. This altar was not for a sin offering but for a burnt offering. A sin offering is for redemption while a burnt offering is an offering of ourselves to God. The altar here does not refer to the Lord Jesus' crucifixion and death for us; it refers to the consecration of ourselves to God. It was the kind of altar spoken of in Romans 12:1. The mercy of God caused the Lord Jesus to die for us. And the mercy of God provided the cross on which we died with him and on which the devil was dealt with. By the mercy of God, we have his life within, and by his mercy, he brings us into his glory. And we move from glory to more glory.

God wants everything whole; he doesn't want a half offering. He can't accept anything less than absolute and complete consecration. And by building the altar, Abram was pledging his complete consecration to Yahweh. For what purpose was the burnt offering placed on the altar? It was to be wholly burned. Many of us think that we offer ourselves to God so that we can do this or that for him, but what he wants from us is a burning. He wants to consume us, his sacrifice, on his altar of love. He wants us to offer ourselves to him and be burned for him, become his living sacrifices, and live a life completely for God.

This altar would acknowledge Abram's thankfulness to God for his promise and act as a commitment to love, serve, and worship him. When God comes to us, an altar of worship becomes the true response of love to him. The altar shows that we're on earth only for God. He's our life, so we put everything on the altar. The Babel-builders made a tower and a name for themselves while Abraham made an altar and called on the name of the Lord. God promised that he would make Abram's name famous or great, but here we see Abram making God's name famous or great.

Wherever Abram had a tent, he had an altar. The tent-life of separation is sure to produce an altar of heavenly fellowship. An altar means we keep nothing for ourselves and give all to God. While Abram lived in a tent without foundations, he was looking and waiting for a city with unshakeable foundations (Hebrews 11:10). Likewise we are living in the "tent"[8] of church life today, waiting for its ultimate consummation as the New Jerusalem, the City of God with unshakeable foundations.

As Abram dwelt in the tent, he lived in the shadow of the New

Jerusalem, the eternal tabernacle. Abram's tent was the seed that grew into the tabernacle of the congregation, found in the book of Exodus, with its harvest being the New Jerusalem. Even though God promised him the land, Abram looked for the Eternal City. Someday Abraham will say to the Lord, *I remember the day you came to my tent; now you have made us your tent.*

Abram must not look at the Canaanites dwelling in the land but the promise of God. Instead of occupying ourselves with Satan's power to keep us from our inheritance, God calls us to trust Christ's power to bring us in. Instead of indulging in a spirit of fear, Abram walked in a spirit of worship. He could enjoy the promise of God, and that was enough. This faith led him to build the altar of praise to the Promise Keeper.

The Bible nowhere promises us that our circumstances will always be pleasing and comfortable. Ours is the peace of God, not the peace of circumstances. We are never to judge the rightness of our path by the presence of trials. The path of obedience will always be a test to our flesh. Abram built his altar while surrounded by his enemies. Paul was called to Philippi by a supernatural vision, yet the first thing he encountered was a prison cell.

ABRAM'S ALTAR AT BETHEL

How significant this is! Abram pitched his tent between two places, Bethel and Ai. The names of these locations are significant. *Bethel* means "the house of God," and *Ai* means "a heap of ruins." This is clearly a time of decision for Abram. He must turn his back on one or the other. As he journeyed toward the promise, the house of God was before him, and a heap of ruins behind him.

Where have you pitched your tent today? Have you left the heap of ruins and turned your gaze toward the house of God? The house of God is drawing us in. Our old life was just a heap of ruins, and we have stepped into our resurrection life. There's nothing to go back to, and there was never anything of value there anyway. It was just a heap of ruins. It is time to experience all that God has in store for us as we walk into our new creation life in the house of God. He is in this place of Bethel. And God is bringing us, his people, into the revelation of the house of God.

When we come into his abiding place and call on the name of Yahweh, we show our utter dependence on him. He is our strength. Worship is not just sounds coming out of our mouths, but it's a walk, a lifestyle of dependence upon the Lord. Abram built an altar of worship and called out to the strength that comes from the name of the Lord. You can call out to him today, and you will find his strength and peace flooding your heart.

LET'S PRAY

Mighty God, I come to hide myself in you, my strength. So many times you have healed my heart and drawn me back to you. I build an altar of worship in my heart today. No matter what is happening around me, within me I will worship you. You are the God who answers my prayer every time I turn to you. I love you, my God, and I give my heart of praise. Amen.

6

During Tests of Faith, Turn to God

At that time, a severe famine struck the land of Canaan, forcing Abram to travel down to Egypt.... He said to his wife Sarai, "Look, I'm worried because I know that you are a beautiful, gorgeous woman. When the Egyptian men take one look at you, they will say, 'She is his wife.' Then they will kill me in order to have you. Just tell them you are my sister so that they will treat me well...and spare my life."

Genesis 12:10–13

Abram's Failure in Egypt

Failure is something we all can relate to. Many times I have had to place the memories of my failures back into the empty tomb.

Every one of God's chosen will have a failure in his or her past. We can trace most of our failures back to letting go of faith and doing something in our own strength, following our own desires. Faith always faces tests. Abram entered into his time of testing in the form of a famine. So often when we set out to our promised land, we encounter a famine. You can be right where God wants you to be and still face severe trials. But it's always better to suffer while on God's path than to be at ease in Satan's wilderness. This was quite a test for Abram. Would he stay in the land where God had led him? Abram journeyed all the way from Chaldea to Canaan on the bare word of the Lord. Would he trust God now in the time of need or turn to Egypt (Habakkuk 3:17–18)? Egypt is a figurative picture of alliance with the world.

To go down into Egypt is to depend on the arm of flesh. "Woe to those who run down to Egypt for help…Their confident trust is not in the Holy One of Israel, nor do they consult with Yahweh" (Isaiah 31:1). Just as Adam chose the wrong path and brought the entire human race into sin's darkness, Abram's wrong choice to go to Egypt brought about an entire nation's enslavement to Egypt during the days of Moses. Not only that, but Abram's grandson Jacob would also revisit the sin of his grandfather and would be taken down to Egypt because of famine in the land.

Several similarities exist between Abram and Moses both going into Egypt. Abraham finds a way out with his "sister" Sarah, and so does Moses when his sister also saves him. Miriam hides the baby Moses among the reeds of the Nile. In a way, Israel's redemption began with a sister. Pharaoh takes Sarah into his Egyptian household where he intends to enslave her in his harem, and another pharaoh will take the Jewish people into his home, where they will remain enslaved for four hundred years. To intervene in the case of Sarah's enslavement, God sends a plague to Pharaoh's people, and when God put an end to Israel's enslavement, he sent ten plagues to break the bondage of his people. Pharaoh sent Abram away with gifts, making him wealthy. When the pharaoh in Moses's time sent Moses away with the people (Pharaoh's former slaves), they, too, carried off wealth: vessels of silver and gold.

There is no mention of Abram building an altar in Egypt, for Egypt was not a place of breakthrough but a place of compromise. One compromise led to another. For it was while he was in Egypt that he lied about his wife. He protected himself by claiming she was his sister. He had more confidence in his scheme than in God's grace.

FAILURE, THE BACK DOOR TO SUCCESS

> When Pharaoh's dignitaries spotted [Sarai], they went to Pharaoh and raved about her beauty. Then they took Sarai into the palace and made her part of Pharaoh's harem. Because she pleased Pharaoh, Abram got along very well in Egypt and received royal treatment: he was given sheep, cattle, male and female donkeys, camels, and male and female slaves.

> But Yahweh struck Pharaoh and his household with terrible diseases because he had taken Abram's wife, Sarai. So Pharaoh sent for Abram and said, "How could you do this to me? Why didn't you tell me she was your wife? And why did you lie to me by saying, 'She's my sister,' so that I took her as my wife? Now, here's your wife back; take her and begone!" Then Pharaoh gave strict orders to his men to escort them out of Egypt. (Genesis 12:15–20)

Abram's sin was a poor example to his wife, to those who accompanied him, and to Pharaoh. He cared only for himself and did not trust God to protect him. The fear of man brought a snare to his soul as it does with all of us. His fears were hypothetical and his ethics situational. Although known for his faith, Abram fell through unbelief even though God had appeared to him twice. In the description of Abraham in Hebrews 11, this fall is left out. Because God is gracious, it only mentions Abram's faith.

Sarai must have been a beautiful woman. Remarkable since she was nearly sixty-five years old! And so, Pharaoh was advised by others to take beautiful Sarai as a concubine. In the culture of that day, Pharaoh had to purchase her. To gain his consent, Pharaoh gave Abram sheep, cattle, donkeys, camels, and servants. The wealth of the sinners was laid up for the just. Even in his compromise, God blessed Abram. Our faith fails, but God's never does.

Somehow, perhaps by a dream, God showed Pharaoh his sin. He rebuked Abram for lying about his wife, and he sent him away in peace. Enriched with the spoils of Egypt, Abram returns to the promised land. This was more than just a lesson on honesty; God was preventing Abram and Sarai from deserting his promise of a chosen nation that they would one day birth. Their offspring would be holy, not perverted by Sarai becoming part of Pharaoh's harem. God was protecting the future of the covenant.

In Egypt there was no tent, no altar, no calling on the name of the Lord. Abram's time in Egypt was wasted time. It was a detour from the purpose of God. It led to compromise and sin. It was during their stay in Egypt that Sarai took her the maid, Hagar, and gave her to Abram (Genesis 16:3). Hagar brought strife, jealousy, and trouble into Abram's household. If they hadn't gone to Egypt, they wouldn't have had Hagar, for Hagar was an Egyptian. If they hadn't taken Hagar, there would have been no Ishmael. Beware of going down to Egypt when you are tested. Learn to trust and not be moved when the famine is all around you.

Yet in spite of Abram's failure, he left Egypt with even more wealth than he came with. God's blessing did not lift off Abram's life because of one failure, nor will God lift his blessing off your life because of the mess you're in. Messes become miracles; just wait—you'll see.

LET'S PRAY

Almighty God, you are always with me. Your hand of love will guide me even when I fail. You are so kind and gracious to me. I never want to wander from your love. Lead me forward into the fulness of your purpose for me. I am yours forever! Amen.

7

BE AN EXAMPLE,
NOT AN ECHO

Abram took his wife and all that he owned, and left Egypt. They
returned to the southern desert region, and Lot went with them.
Now Abram had become very rich.

GENESIS 13:1–2

ABRAM HAD A LOT TO LOSE

I'm so thankful God lets us start over. The detour will bring
us back to the main road. Abram starts over until he retraces his
steps and once again finds the place of blessing, where his tent
had once been. It was at Bethel that Abram decided to leave the
place of anointing and go down to Egypt. And now he returns
with humility of heart to rebuild his altar of devotion. And so it

is with us; there are many times when we must return to our first love and re-examine our commitment to follow the Lord. Abram had an altar to return to, a place where his fellowship with the Father could be restored. Abram knew where to go to be restored and to find God again.

It was at the altar that Abram called on the name of the Lord. It was there that God restored Abram to the place of sweet communion and fellowship once again (Psalm 23:3). His faith was not in a plan but in a person. His desire for Yahweh meant more to him than any other desire. The grace of God shines brightly even in Abram's trip to Egypt. Abram returns with a broken heart but also with the wealth and spoils of the land. Blessed with possessions, Abram became a very wealthy man (literal Hebrew "heavy").

Lot, Abram's nephew, also amassed livestock, servants, and possessions. It seems even those who hung out with Abram were blessed. And so Lot lived off Abram's blessing. It's not enough to follow in the tracks of someone who is blessed because we must discover our own track of blessing and fruitfulness in God. Nothing will endure unless it's of God. Our borrowed blessings will fail if we fail to have our own link with the living God.

Lot was only an echo, not an example. He saw the faith of Abram but could not hear the voice of God for himself. He was along for the ride. Nothing can be more worthless than an imitation. Are you walking under a divine influence or a human influence? The blessing of someone else won't prop us up. The call of God hadn't reached Lot's heart. He left Ur with Abram but fell in the plains of Sodom. The blessing of God had not filled his vision.

A DISPUTE BETWEEN ABRAM AND LOT

> Now Lot, who accompanied Abram, was also rich and
> had accumulated flocks, herds, family, and servants.
> Arguments erupted between Abram's herdsmen and Lot's
> herdsmen because the land could not support both living
> together, for their animals and possessions were too
> numerous. (Genesis 13:5–7)

Why didn't Lot speak to his herdsmen and correct them? Was
the strife between Abram's herdsmen and Abram the real problem? Lot's failure to cultivate friendship with God caused his
backsliding. The strife of the herdsmen and Lot's failure to honor
Abram by neglecting to step in to correct the situation was just a
manifestation of Lot's worldliness.

The Hebrew word *Lot* means "covert," "secret," or "concealed."
Lot hid everything about himself away in his heart. He lived a
life of compromise. And so the secret tug of the world drew him
away from the place of blessing. He had never really left Ur; he
remained an idolater at heart. He looked for the closest thing that
resembled Egypt when he chose the rich plains. He chose what
would please himself without considering the consequences. But
fires of judgment eventually burned his possessions, and he ended
up living in a cave. So much for protecting his stuff.

Abram's words displayed the "meekness of wisdom" (James
3:13 NKJV). Lot would have had nothing if it had not been for
Abram. He could have told Lot to leave. But he willingly deferred
to his nephew for the sake of keeping peace. He loved God and
hated strife. It was not compromise for him to defer; it was wisdom. They were relatives, and they had an incredible blessing and

a vast inheritance they could have shared. Yet instead of sharing, Lot's herdsmen quarreled, and Lot failed to intervene.

> At that time, Canaanites and Perizzites were also in the land. So Abram said to Lot, "Let's not quarrel with each other, or between our herdsmen, since we are relatives. Look at the vast land that is in front of you! Let's settle in different regions. If you choose the land on the left, then I'll go right, and if you want land on the right, then I'll go left." (Genesis 13:7–9)

Why would they quarrel in the presence of the Canaanites and Perizzites? Why would brethren contend with one another before the lost of this world? Couldn't God, the God of heaven and all the earth, give them wisdom to settle their difficulty without a humiliating argument before the unbelievers?

Abram looked at the situation from God's viewpoint. This is why he could choose the path of peace over the path of personal rights. Abram took what was left. He refused to war with his family member and turned from the strife. The way of peace is a pleasant way, although it may cost us in the short term. This is the way of faith. God had already promised him the land, so he knew that he needed to let it go and needed to wait for God's perfect timing. He had already made the mistake once before. He ran ahead of God and birthed Ishmael, trying to make God's promise happen ahead of God's timing. He did not want to make that mistake again. Abram surrendered control and let God be his inheritance.

God will always treat you better than men when you leave the choice up to him. And the portion God chooses for you will satisfy you (Psalm 16:5–6; 84:11). What security faith brings to the heart! Trust in God and rest in his goodness. As a friend of God, Abram would later be given all of the land as his inheritance.

Abram is a picture of the man of the Spirit:

- He walked in wisdom.

- He had love for his brother without prejudice.

- He valued unity.

- He was concerned about his witness to the heathen.

- He gave up his own rights and desires for wealth.

- He chose a tent and enjoyed fellowship with God.

Let's Pray

My heavenly Father, I want the faith of Abraham. Give me your power to live in the steps of Abraham. Each step of my journey, I want to please you. Guide me, teach me, and correct me when I need it. I trust your heart of kindness is always toward me. No one has been as kind to me as you. I love you, Father. I want to walk with you today. Amen.

8

BEWARE OF SEEKING THE WORLD

*"If you choose the land on the left, then I'll go right,
and if you want land in the right, then I'll go left."*

GENESIS 13:9

A LOT OF MISTAKES

Abram was quite generous. Lot, in his greed, took full advantage of it. The flesh of man is opportunistic. We are graspers by nature. To yield and defer to others is a work of the Spirit of God within us. Lot looked over the land and chose Sodom, the place destined for judgment. Lot chose the world. He walked by sight, what looked good to the eyes (1 John 2:15–17). Lot was led astray and left the place of blessing to go into the place of judgment.

Lot became an official of Sodom seated at its gate (Genesis 19:1). But he gained virtually nothing by separating from Abram. Nothing at all. The men of Sodom polluted him. Instead of Lot bringing light into Sodom, darkness entered his soul (2 Peter 2:7–8). Lot is a picture of a believer who lives far below his calling and destiny. He preferred the well-watered plains to Abram's altar. By wrong choices and subtle compromises, we bring many sorrows into our lives. Beware of seeking to make the best of both worlds. Seek first his kingdom.

When Abram offered the choice to Lot, he should have said, "Uncle, the choice is yours. God is with you. So my choice is your choice." Too often the younger person likes to be separated from the older generation. By separating himself from the called one, Abram, Lot did not follow the will of God. When we align ourselves with those who walk with God, we receive protection that we cannot receive elsewhere. Our flesh would rather DIY ("do it yourself"), but God wants us to walk in fellowship with called ones.

It was God's purpose to separate Abram from his land of birth, from his kinsmen, from every earthly attachment. In the separation of Abram and Lot, God's purpose is finally realized. Abram had a *Lot* to lose. Now Abram is left alone with God.

GOD'S PROMISE TO FAITHFUL ABRAM

After Lot separated from him, Yahweh spoke to Abram, "Lift up your eyes and look around you to the north, the south, the east, and the west. As far as you can see in every direction is the land that I will give to you forever.... I will multiply [your seed] until they are as numerous as the specks of dust on the earth. If anyone could count the dust of the earth, then your offspring could also be counted. Now, get up and walk through the land—its length and its breadth. All the land you walk upon will be my gift to you!" (Genesis 13:14–17)

Alone with God, Abram receives another divine visitation. God tells Abram to lift up his eyes and look at his inheritance. Lot lifted up his physical eyes (v. 10), but Abram lifted up his spiritual eyes and saw that it was better to wait than to strive. Abram waited for God to give him the land, but Lot took it for himself.

A new Abram was emerging as he put his personal self-interest behind him. When we read the account of his life, we see no desire coming from him to preserve his pride or position. He uses his spiritual authority to bless and to give, and his personal rights take the back seat to his testimony before the Canaanites. God had worked deeply in his heart. God tied together the promise of the land and the promise of offspring. God compares the vast number of his future offspring to the dust of the earth. It would be his offspring who would ultimately inherit the land of promise, including the land chosen by Lot.

It was as if God were saying, *Abraham, the real secret to birthing your dream is for you to see it. I want you to see it, and I want you to dream it. If you can see and you can dream it, then you can have it!* Receiving a true prophetic word can begin a time of dreaming that can influence the future. As Abram walked through the land, he would see the vast extent of the promises of God. The One who prepared the holy land will prepare the holy seed.

Abram moved his tents. In anticipation of more from God, he ventured forth in faith. He was willing to be a pilgrim that always had to move his tents when fresh revelation came. The pain of strife and separation gave way to a fresh revelation of the promise. Notice the progression of verse eighteen: "Abram moved his camp and settled by the oaks of Mamre, which are at Hebron, and there he built another altar to Yahweh."

Here are four realities that are a part of every Abrahamic journey:

- *Obedience*—"Abram moved his camp." To go with God means we are always willing to move, to change, and to advance.

- *Anointing*—*Mamre* means "fatness" and represents the place of anointing. To go with God means we will step into his favor and presence. We will dwell in a place of abundance and overflow.

- *Fellowship*—*Hebron* means "fellowship or communion." To go with God means we will walk in fellowship with him. He will share his secrets with those who love him.

- *Worship*—Abram "built another altar to the Lord." To go with God means a life of continual worship. We will build one breakthrough altar after another.

The chapter ends as it began with Abram building an altar to the Lord at the place of the anointing. Lot chose Sodom, but Abram chose the Lord. As a worshiper, he had responded correctly to strife and waited patiently for the Lord to fulfill his promise. From the beginning of the journey Abram was a man of devotion to God. And with every step his friendship with God was growing deeper and sweeter. He had become a man of faith, far ahead of his time, an example to all his "spiritual seed." Abram had learned about the faithfulness of God, and now he was ready for what was about to come—a battle.

Let's Pray

Father, I choose you over anything the world may offer me. I resolve to follow you anytime, anywhere as you lead me. I choose to make my days joyful, even at a clouded dawn. Fill my day with a selfless love for others, especially my family. Make me a servant of all, and give me a heart that will never be offended if I'm slighted, overlooked, or misunderstood. Help me never to force others to surrender to my desires or opinions. Give me new visions today of your truth, justice, and holiness. Surround my soul with your protection, and deliver me from every temptation to turn to my way and not yours. I want to keep my heart clean, but I need your grace. Keep me unscarred from meanness, selfishness, and dishonesty. Give me your hatred of sin and your love for others. Make me to be a cup of strength to the suffering, a voice of peace to the troubled, and an example of love to the straying. In the strong and holy name of my Lord and Savior Jesus Christ. Amen.

9

RESTORE THOSE OVERTAKEN WITH A FAULT

During the reign of Amraphel, king of Babylon, he allied with three other kings: Arioch king of Ellasar, Kedorlaomer king of Elam, and Tidal king of Goyim. These four kings went to war against five kings: Bera king of Sodom, Birsha king of Gomorrah, Shinab king of Admah, Shemeber king of Zeboiim, and the king of Bela, which is Zoar.

GENESIS 14:1–2

WORLD WAR I

This chapter opens with the first war mentioned in Scripture. Four kings went to war against five kings. All of them ruled over powerful city-states. And the territory they fought over was the trade route of Egypt that the four eastern states had to pass through. Whoever controlled this land bridge would have a monopoly on international commerce.

As the battle raged, Lot was taken captive. He had laid up treasures on earth only to have thieves break in and steal them. But one of Lot's servants escaped and brought Abram the news of his nephew's captivity. Abram could have responded, "That's his problem. He made a wrong choice, and now he'll have to pay the price and suffer for it. Who knows, God may be teaching him a lesson!" No, Abram had no root of bitterness. And instead he moved with compassion and took with him 318 trained servants to rescue Lot and the others who were taken captive. This must also be the way that we respond. When we hear that believers are overtaken with a fault, our first response must be to restore them and to see them healed. It's not our place to condemn and ignore them (Galatians 6:1).

Boldness filled Abram's heart (Proverbs 28:1) as he went into battle for his family member. He didn't hesitate but pursued the conquerors. And he succeeded and brought back Lot, his servants, and all the goods that were stolen. Unlike Cain, Abram became his brother's keeper.

The five kings should have been victorious over the four. But the four kings defeated the five, taking Sodom captive. What happened in the natural with Lot and his family was a picture of what had already happened in his spirit. The spirit of this world held him captive. But Abram had entered the war from a place of fellowship (Hebron). He went into the war with an advantage. Spiritually, he had already joined the winning team.

As believers, we're of Abraham's family, for he is the father of faith. And when he went to battle for the destiny of Lot, he also warred over our destiny. When he warred against the four kings, he battled for his natural seed as well as his future spiritual seed, which is us! Notice the names of the warring kings and lessons we can learn even through their names.

The Names of the Kings

1. King *Amraphel* represents our enemy who speaks lies in an attempt to keep us in darkness, for his name means "speaker of darkness, keeper of god." Hope and peace will never be a part of his vocabulary. During seasons when vision is blocked and we can't discern what's going on in the natural, focus on the supernatural. God's words are superior to anything man has to say. Our enemy will be a speaker of lies, whom we can never trust. Our God is the speaker of truth; indeed, he is the way, the truth, and the life. Don't allow the enemy to lie to you concerning your future. Leave those lies behind and cross over into your promise. Amraphel is the king of *Babylon* ("confusion"). This principality is the author of confusion that brings division into the fellowship of Christ's body. With words spoken in secret and behind your back, the power of this spirit brings confusion and sows discord.

2. King *Arioch* reveals that the devil's strategy comes against you as a roaring lion and causes you to fear, for *Arioch* means "lion-like." But his roar is a lie and his attempts to kill, steal, and destroy are puny compared to the Lion from the tribe of Judah, who is on your side. And he is the One who will direct

you as you cross over into your destined place. The dominion of Arioch was *Ellasar*, an area of ancient Asia that means "revolting from God," "rebellion," or "God is the punisher." The devil may prowl around as a roaring lion, but it's God who will do the punishing, and God will punish him.

3. King *Kedorlaomer* is a spirit of control that comes against you to bind your soul to your past and to keep a victim locked into passivity, for Kedorlaomer's name means "binding up." The way you can defeat a "binding" spirit is to come into agreement with God and his Word. The devil will always seek to limit you and keep you inside the boundaries that he sets. If you're not careful, you'll keep focusing on your past failure and limit God to only what you're familiar or comfortable with. And you'll not be able to step out into the unknown. And you'll fail to cross over into your future. Kedorlaomer was the king of *Elam*, which is the ancient word for Persia or modern-day Iran. *Elam* also can mean "secrets" and is a picture of false religious structures, secret rites, etc. We must become a people of purpose who realize that what we do really does affect eternal purposes. We not only shape our own future but also the eternal condition of our own soul, our cities, and others by binding up this strongman when we focus on God's Word and not on past failures.

4. King *Tidal* is that foe that comes against you to make you shrink back and crawl away, intimidated and weak, for *Tidal* means "fearsome, to make afraid" and "to shrink back and crawl away." Doesn't this sound like a tactic of the devil against us today? Satan would love to see us shrink back from our God-given assignments. Tidal is the king of *Goiim* or "peoples," or, in other words, intimidation and the fear of man. Any time we walk in the fear of man, we'll shrink back and crawl away from our destiny. The enemy wants to keep us in fear so that we won't pursue what the Father has set before us. He wants us to fear our future rather than allow God to use us as nation changers and history makers. And rather than realize that this is your time of victory and favor, he wants to seduce you to believe the very opposite. So be on guard and press forward into your new authority. Don't shrink back or crawl away. Your appointed time of favor has come.

These kings in the land represented the spiritual powers keeping Abram from his inheritance. They were dark powers sent to rob him of his destiny and hinder the blessing. But Abram had learned the principles of spiritual warfare and fought for the blessings of others. In this way, Abram becomes a picture of a true intercessor.

ABRAM RESCUES LOT

They captured Lot, Abram's nephew who had been living in Sodom, and took him and all his possessions.... When Abram heard that his nephew Lot had been taken captive by the four kings, he mobilized all the men in his camp, 318 in all who had been born and trained in his own household, and he pursued the invaders as far north as Dan. Then, during the night, Abram strategically divided his forces and defeated them. His forces attacked them and routed them as far as Hobah, north of Damascus. He recovered all the stolen possessions and brought back his nephew Lot, together with the women and all the prisoners. (Genesis 14:12, 14–16)

The patriarch Abram takes his own personal army of 318 disciples, who were trained in his own house (local church), and won a great victory. What a bold step of faith to take only 318 men against the kings and their expert armies of war! Abram moved under divine favor knowing that God was with him. We, too, have this favor upon us and must act in faith when we see a brother trapped in sin. We must rise up to do battle for him. Abram felt the burden to bring his nephew back. He chased the kings to a place called "Hobah," or "hiding place." Overcomers are those who recover all that the enemy has taken. We must go into every hiding place of darkness until all is restored.

Abram, the man of faith, conquered the kings of the land. He was victorious and truly crossed over into his inheritance by faith. And as he did, he rescued many. The blessing of Abraham made him a blessing to others. We, too, as sons and daughters of Abraham, must battle with some kings. The kings in our mind, the kings in our emotions, and kings over our will. And after we have vanquished "the kings," our Melchizedek will come to meet with us, celebrating our victory. When we are victorious, Christ will manifest. Today Christ, our Melchizedek, is interceding in heaven for us overcoming ones.

Let's Pray

Glorious God, I love your ways! You have trained me and prepared me to fulfill your purposes. You will make my life a blessing to others. Make me one who will consider others to the point where I put their needs above my own. Help me rescue the hurting. Make me a healer of those around me. Let me bring joy and blessing into my family. I trust you to live through me today—until the blessing on my life blesses others. Amen.

10

GOD'S LOVE
IS ALL WE NEED

*After Abram returned from defeating Kedorlaomer and the kings
who were with him, the king of Sodom went out to meet Abram
at the Valley of the Shaveh (known as the King's Valley). And
Melchizedek, who was both a priest of the Most High God and the
king of Salem, brought out to Abram bread and wine. He spoke
over him a special blessing, saying, "Blessed is Abram by God Most
High, Creator of heaven and earth. And blessed be God Most High,
whose power delivered your enemies into your hands."*

GENESIS 14:17–20

MELCHIZEDEK, PRIEST OF GOD MOST HIGH

As Abram returns from battle, two kings come out to meet him: the king of Sodom offering the spoils of war and the king of Salem,[9] Melchizedek, bringing bread and wine. This is so deeply significant and affects Abram powerfully for the rest of his life.[10] Overwhelmed with the revelation of who God is and the victory God won for him, Abram abandons all to the Lord.

After a great victory, a temptation followed. This victory for Abram was both a temptation and a revelation: a temptation to take things and a revelation of God Most High. This is the time that Melchizedek comes to Abram while the king of Sodom wants to reward Abram. What a picture! The king of Sodom is willing to give Abram all he wants of the goods of this world. And this meant that Abram could have come into considerable wealth. But at the same time here comes the king of Salem, ready to bless Abram in the name of El Elyon, God Most High!

The material goods of Sodom might have made Abram's life comfortable, but instead, Abram chose the "bread and wine" that refreshed his spirit. And the royal priest, Melchizedek, presented to Abram the blessing of El Elyon, God Most High, Creator of heaven and earth, the God of all fullness within the veil. Abram is blessed in this new revelation of who God was and is. And this all took place in the King's Valley, the low place, the place where we meet the true King, the King of all kings.

Who was Melchizedek, this priest-king of Salem who prophesied blessing to Abram? Hebrew tradition states he was Shem, survivor of the flood and the oldest living man. Most Bible students believe that Melchizedek was a Christophany or a pre-incarnation appearance of the Lord Jesus Christ, our Priest and our King. Melchizedek came from Salem, which means "peace." Jesus is our King of peace. He came from a Salem that is not of this earth but from a heavenly realm (Galatians 4:26; Psalm 110:4; Hebrews 7:23–24). Abram had a face-to-face encounter with Jesus Christ, the Son of God! The friend of God met the Son of God.

The priesthood of Aaron was an earthly priesthood that was always interrupted by death. For the sons of Aaron would continually take the priesthood only to die and pass the mantle to another. But Jesus died once and for all, and he now rules as a High Priest after the order of Melchizedek over both Jew and gentiles (Hebrews 7:2). He is our true Priest and walks in royal authority as our King of righteousness. (The name *Melchizedek* means "my king is righteous.")

The priesthood of Melchizedek was truly unique. No genealogy is given for him. He is without beginning and without ending (v. 3). Abram didn't bless Melchizedek, but Melchizedek blessed Abram. This king of Salem steps out of history to reveal El Elyon to victorious Abram. This was the Ancient of Days, the King of the ages, the I AM, the One who lives to make continual intercession for us. He was our Great High Priest after the order of Melchizedek. This priesthood receives tithes of all (v. 4). In paying of tithes to Melchizedek, Abram acknowledged God's grace in giving him the victory.

Melchizedek was a priest on behalf of whom? Not the Jews, for Abram was yet to have a son. It was on behalf of the gentiles. God established a priesthood over the *gentiles* before he established a priesthood over the Jews. Melchizedek was a gentile king over a gentile city. This says to me that God had gentiles in his heart even in Genesis. This gentile king came with a revelation of God to impart to Abram. This mysterious gentile priest blessed the father of many nations. As Creator of heaven and earth, God is over the nations, not just Abram and his clan. This Most High God has given an inheritance to all peoples (Deuteronomy 32:8; Daniel 4:17).

Melchizedek came to Abram because of the victory he had won over the kings. He wanted to nourish the victor with bread and wine. Isn't this just like the Lord Jesus? He comes to us when we are battle weary. And he not only refreshes our spirits, but he also prepares us for our next level of conflict. With a fresh glimpse into his heart, we're filled with grace to encounter the enemy once again. The next time you're tempted, remember the mercies of our Lord Jesus, Possessor of heaven and earth. He is always ready to nourish you with the bread of heaven and Holy Spirit power to overcome.

ABRAM PAYS TITHES TO MELCHIZEDEK

> Abram gave Melchizedek a tenth of all he possessed. Then the king of Sodom said to Abram, "Just give me the people you rescued; keep all the spoils for yourself." But Abram said to the king of Sodom, "I raised my hand to Yahweh, God Most High, and I pledged a solemn oath to the Possessor of heaven and earth that I would keep nothing for myself that belongs to you, not even a thread of a garment or sandal strap. That way, you will never be able to say, 'I was the one that made Abram rich.'" (Genesis 14:20–23)

Abram's victory produced a remarkable thing in him. He saw God in a new way. And he acknowledges this revelation by giving Melchizedek a "tithe," or "tenth," of all the spoils of the battle (Hebrews 7:4). All the while the king of Sodom stood there and witnessed it all. He watched Abram give over a tenth of all he possessed to this mysterious priest.

Then the king of Sodom offered to give Abram all the spoils of the war. But the blessing of El Elyon gave Abram strength to refuse the king of Sodom's offer. Abram had found a higher love.

God had imparted something to Abram that made the things of this life seem like nothing. Abram saw that the God of heaven and earth loved him, and this was all he needed.

But as for Lot, there is no mention that he ever thanked Abram for his rescue or that he ever built an altar of gratitude to God. Lot was a man of the world and went back to Sodom. But Abram's testimony was, "I raised my hand to Yahweh, God Most High, and I pledged a solemn oath to the Possessor of heaven and earth that I would keep nothing for myself." This God would now be his source and provider. A blessed man does not need the world's help. God is enough. Abram went to war in the power of that name. The power to overcome the world was in his faith in his God Most High (1 John 5:4). The goods of Sodom were nothing compared to the revelation of God's love for him. The bread and wine were an invitation from God to feast on him, not on the things of this life. Nothing else would have Abram's affection.

Abram refused to be enriched by the king of Sodom. How could Abram be a deliverer if he himself was not delivered? This was the path of separation that was always before Abram. Would God be enough? Could he leave it all behind? May the Lord keep us all true to our God in these days of snares and compromises.

LET'S PRAY

My heart cries out to you, God, my wonderful King. You are everything to me. You mean more to me than any possession or relationship I have. You have given me more than enough. I have all that I need. My dreams and desires are fulfilled in you today. I love you, my Father and my God. Amen.

11

HAVE A HEAVENLY VISION
FOR YOUR LIFE

Afterwards, the word of Yahweh came to Abram in a vision and said, "Abram, don't yield to fear, for I am your Faithful Shield and your Abundant Reward."
But Abram replied, "Lord Yahweh, what good is your reward if I remain childless? I'm about to die without a son, and my servant, Eliezer of Damascus, will inherit all my wealth. A servant in my household will end up with everything because you have not given me any children."
Immediately, the word of Yahweh came to him: "No! Eliezer will not be your heir. I will give you a son from your own body to be your heir." Then Yahweh brought him outside his tent and said, "Gaze into the night sky. Go ahead and try to count the stars." He continued, "Your seed will be as numerous as the stars!" And

THE BLESSING

Abram trusted every word Yahweh had spoken! And because of his faith, Yahweh credited it to him as righteousness.

GENESIS 15:1–6

A HEAVENLY VISION

Because he rejected the things of Sodom, Abram is granted a fresh revelation of God as his faithful shield and abundant reward. Abram had discovered that it was better to be hidden behind Jehovah's shield than to take refuge in the things of the world. Knowing God as his reward was infinitely better than whatever Abram lost. God is our faithful shield that we might rest in him and our abundant reward that is worth waiting for. God came to Abram in a vision and promised to be his defender. In tender grace, he brought peace and rest to the heart of his friend.

Abram was looking for a city whose architect and builder was God. And so, he declined to take even a shoelace from Sodom. God more than makes it up to Abram. He is compensated with a new revelation: the revelation that God is his shield and his great reward.

God wants to fill our future with himself. He promised Abram that he would be more than a rewarder; he would be his very abundant reward. Life's greatest treasure is the knowledge of God. What greater pleasure is there than intimacy with our Father God as our very great reward? True rewards are found in him alone, not in the favor of others. Others will view us in light of our weakness, but God sees us in light of our destiny. Our true identity is wrapped up in God who understands every movement of our heart. He is our great reward.

Abram was a wise intercessor. When he received this word of favor, he took the opportunity to ask his Sovereign Lord for a

70

child. This was a prayer of faith, for Abram wanted his promised son. He had heard this promise before, but where was the son? He had waited ten years in the land already. And all he had in his household was Eliezer of Damascus. Why had God taken so long? We are so prone to mistake delays for denials. But God uses delays to instruct us, break us, and to leave us dependent upon him alone. We tend to want to trust anything but God. At times, we're left with nothing but his promise. Will we believe when all we have is the word of the Lord?

Under the prevailing custom of the day, if Abram died childless, his household servant would become his heir. But what about the promise of offspring? The inheritance must come to a son, not a servant. Sonship is the basis of inheritance (Galatians 4:6–7). He had received the Word of the Lord with the promise, *I will give you a son from your own body to be your heir.*

Abram was then given a prophetic sign as Yahweh took him outside his tent to gaze at the heavens and count the stars. Each star he saw would represent an heir, a descendant. This prophetic gesture had a profound effect on Abram. He spoke to the One who made the sky. From that moment on, he believed the Lord, and "because of his faith, Yahweh credited it to him as righteousness." This encounter with the Sovereign Lord changed his destiny forever. He no longer considered the impossibility of having a child. And God counted this faith as an equivalent of righteousness. God was pleased with his friend. Abram believed that God would give him a son, and we know and believe that God has already given us his Son, Jesus Christ. Our faith is likewise counted as righteousness. We're heirs of Abraham's blessing and all the blessings of Jesus Christ. God sees us as righteous as Jesus Christ!

In Genesis 13:14–17, God used the dust of the land as a

prophetic sign. And in chapter fifteen, he used the heavenly stars. Both the dust (earthly seed) and the stars (heavenly seed) point us to the true descendants of Abraham. And so the church (Jew and gentile) is the spiritual Israel (Galatians 3:26–29). The sand on the seashore and the stars of the skies both speak of the power of God to raise up sons and daughters that love him and believe his promise. The seed will be a corporate people on this earth.

The faith of Abraham is the kind of faith that is precious to God. It's the kind of faith that believes that God will work in and through us to bring forth Christ, the seed. It's entirely God's work and grace through faith that fulfills the promise. All we have is Eliezer, and all we can do in our flesh is Ishmael, but neither of them count for the fulfillment of God's purpose. It must be God himself. After we have truly become nothing, God will work in us to bring forth Christ as the seed, and we will live in him as our land.

This heavenly gaze widened Abram's vision, and he began to see the supernatural in a new way. From then on, he would watch the power of the One who created the stars fulfilling the promise. Abram went from his limited tent vision into unlimited heavenly vision (Ephesians 5:14). It's time for your vision to be expanded too. It's time for you to have your own heavenly vision for your life.

Abram's faith released a fresh revelation. The Lord reminded him of who had redeemed him, the One who was guiding his life (Isaiah 29:2). Faithful was the One who called him. And he would also be faithful to bring him into the land (1 Thessalonians 5:24). Abram experienced a season of growing between being "brought out" and being "given the land." As a pilgrim, he learned to trust in God along the way. Are you learning to trust him on your journey?

Let's Pray

My wonderful God, you have been faithful to me. You lead me in your steps of righteousness for your name's sake. You bring me to the quiet brooks of bliss where I can be restored and refreshed. I am grateful to serve you and call you my Father. Work in my heart today to cling to you and not my past nor my pain. I want only you, especially this day. Amen.

12

GOD BLESSES
ALL WHO BELIEVE

Then he said to him, "I am Yahweh, who brought you out of the
Babylonian city of Ur, to give you all this land to possess." But
Abram said, "Lord Yahweh, how can I be sure that I can possess
this land for myself?"
Yahweh said to him, "Bring me a heifer, a female goat, and a ram,
each three years old, also a turtledove and a young pigeon." So,
Abram brought the animals to him and killed them. He cut them
in two (except the birds) and laid each half opposite the other in
two rows. Vultures swooped down upon the carcasses, but Abram
stood there and drove the vultures away.
As the heavy veil of night fell, Abram went into a deep state of
sleep, and suddenly a great dreadful darkness surrounded him and
he was filled with fear.

GENESIS 15:7–12

GOD'S PROPHETIC COVENANT WITH ABRAM

Abram is God's friend. His numerous encounters with the God of Glory transformed his life. Friends ask friends for favors. So, being the friend of God, he asks for a sign saying, "How can I be sure that I will have a son?" Abram believed, but he needed reassurance to treasure in his heart. Even the faithful need help. God will ratify his promise to Abram with a unique prophetic picture. God directs Abram to prepare for a sacrifice. Abram asks for a son, and God asks for a sacrifice. God still speaks through the sacrifice of his son as a sign to the nations that God loved the world and provided salvation for all.

Abram presented a heifer, a goat, and a ram, each three years old, along with a dove and a young pigeon to the Lord. He killed the animals and divided them in half. All of these sacrifices represented types or pictures of the Lord Jesus Christ. They were not wild animals but tame, like the Lord Jesus. The Lord Jesus was yielded fully to the Father. The heifer, goat, and ram signify the crucified Christ, for they were cut in half, and Jesus was cut and crucified for us. The young heifer also speaks of Christ's strength and vigor. The goat is the animal used in the sin-offering (Leviticus 4:28; 5:6), and the ram is the animal of consecration and substitution. Jesus was the ram caught in the thicket on Mt. Moriah (Genesis 22:13).

But the two birds were kept alive to signify the resurrection of Christ, the One who ascended into heaven as the Prince of Glory. The birds speak of the One who came down from heaven and was raised again to return to heaven. Two is the number representing witness, so the two living birds (dove and pigeon) bear witness to Christ as the resurrected One living in us and for us. The dividing of these animals speaks of the blood covenant that God presents to humanity. God teaches us how a covenant is to be made with another. By cutting the animals in half (except the birds), he is saying that the promise made has to pass between the hearts and organs and inner being of those who make the covenant. And then it's sealed in blood.

So Abram separated the sacrifices and made a lane or path with the halves of the animals on each side. Then he waited throughout the day for God to move. As he waited, he had to drive away the buzzards and "unclean" birds of prey that were after the carcasses. The birds of prey represent our doubts. This is a picture of the one who receives the promise and must deal with doubts and conflicting thoughts. Like buzzards circling overhead, the enemy comes to steal the promise and the hope of fulfillment from our hearts. We must arise and drive away every fear and lie of the enemy. But the longer we wait, the more numerous the doubts. In the heat of a burning day we can easily grow weary and faint. Be alert to this strategy (Habakkuk 2:3; Lamentations 3:26; Romans 8:25).

As the sun sets, a deep sleep came upon him like a "great darkness." And the heavy veil of night fell. And Abram went into a "trance-like state." It was a form of divine ecstasy much like what happened to Adam (Genesis 2:21), and Abram was filled with awe. The Lord now appears in this surreal setting in a prophetic act to confirm his promise to Abram.

What a picture of waiting on God. We believe the promise, and then we find ourselves passing through the darkness of waiting on God. We are left in the "great darkness" of the fulfillment being out of our control. Only God knows when the promise will be realized. The flesh withers, our strength evaporates, doubts clog our way, and we think: *When will he come through for me?* For those of you holding onto prophetic promises yet to be fulfilled, hear this: Even in your great darkness, deal with your doubts and wait on the Lord. Your faithful God will not disappoint you.

God's Covenant with Abram

> When the sun had set, and it was very dark, there suddenly appeared a smoking firepot and a blazing torch that passed between the split carcasses. On that day, Yahweh entered into covenant with Abram: "I have given this land to your descendants, from the Egyptian border to the great river Euphrates." (Genesis 15:17–18)

Yahweh made an incredible promise to Abram. He promised that Abram would receive the title deed of all the land from Egypt north to the Euphrates. God then confirmed this covenant-promise as a smoking fire pot with a blazing torch appeared and passed majestically between the pieces of the sacrifice, consuming them in holy fire (Judges 6:21; Exodus 19:18; 2 Samuel 22:9; Isaiah 6:4). While Abram slept the Father came and walked between the pieces of his faith, confirming the promise. While Abram slept, the battle was won!

The everlasting covenant, which was planned from eternity, was ratified by the resurrection of our Lord Jesus. All that is left for us to do is to rest and wait. When God walked through the severed pieces of the sacrifice, he made a statement indicating that even when Abram failed to keep the covenant, the price had now been paid for him (and for us). In every dark trial, we, as believers, have the "blazing torch" of Jesus with us as a light shining in a dark place (2 Peter 1:19). He turns night into day and shines brightly upon our path. And we can walk in the light, the light of this blazing torch. The day will come when the blazing torch becomes a bush of fire, then a pillar of fire until, finally, it will come to rest upon the heads of every disciple (Acts 2).

God's promise to Abram, spoken that mysterious night, becomes the "title deed" to the land. He's given the boundaries of the expanse of the land of promise, land occupied by the enemy. Powerful princes will someday be dethroned as they march into the fullness of their inheritance. The God that walked between the sacrifices will walk in the land and conquer their foes (Isaiah 43:1–7). When the Lord established his covenant with Abraham, his flame passed twice through the halves of the animals offered by Abraham. The two passes signified that God would fulfill his part in keeping the covenant, and remarkably, he would be the strength in Abraham to fulfill Abraham's part of the covenant as well.

Today, a restored Israel testifies to God's faithfulness to his covenant with Abraham, Isaac, and Jacob. And it's God's covenant with Abraham, not merely the Israeli military, that preserves Israel in our times. This "covenant of pieces" established Israel as a nation. It is the covenant that God set in place to bond his people by a common bloodline and shared ancestry. God gives the Jewish land to the sons of Abraham by covenant. The covenant binds the Jewish people to their land and to their God.

The agreement the Lord cut with his covenant partner was not only for Abraham, but it extended to Abram's descendants as well. The blessing of God would pass on generationally. God's blessing continues from one generation to the next for all who believe. In order for you to take your inheritance, you must prepare to fight the good fight of faith, for God has given you the "land" of your spiritual inheritance. God has spoken, and the only requirement is that you believe and receive your blessing of inheritance. It's yours for the taking!

LET'S PRAY

God, you have been so kind to me. You have kept every promise you've ever made to me. Today I ask for greater faith to believe and receive your promises. Your blessings are endless, and your promises are faithful. Help me to overcome every challenge to my faith. With your grace, I can rise victorious in all things. I humble my heart before you today and ask for great faith. I receive it now, in Jesus' name. Amen.

13

TRUST IN GOD'S TIMING

Now Sarai had borne no children for Abram. She had an Egyptian
slave girl named Hagar, so Sarai said to Abram, "Please listen.
Since Yahweh has kept me childless, go sleep with my maidservant.
Perhaps through her I can build you a family." Abram listened and
did what Sarai asked.

GENESIS 16:1–2

ISHMAEL

God is faithful to keep his promises but not always in our
preferred timetable. Sarai was barren, childless. In her desperation, she tries to nudge the arm of God and convince her husband
into fathering a child with her servant, Hagar. This was a test for
Abram, for he had waited so long for the promised son. In chapter
fifteen, Abram listens to the voice of God, and in chapter sixteen,

he listens to the voice of Sarai. All of this is an example of the wisdom of the flesh, not the wisdom of God. Faith can wait and rest until God fulfills the promise. The flesh has to make it happen anyway it can.

Notice how many times Abram's faith is tested. First his faith had to overcome *the ties to the natural*, for God's call took him away from his country and his kindred. Shortly after arriving in Canaan, Abram's faith was tested by *severe circumstances*—there was famine in the land. Then he faced a painful trial of *strife with family* (his nephew, Lot), which ultimately led to a separation. Later, the Lord tested his *courage* and love for Lot when the enemy captured Lot and he needed rescuing. A test over Abram's *desire for wealth* came when the king of Sodom tempted him with the spoils of battle. He had overcome all of these tests, but now we see him giving in to the suggestion of his wife to *take things into his own hands* when God had seemingly forgotten his promise.

Take another look at this pattern and realize that you, too, will be tested in the very same things. Remember: these are tests that God's favored ones will pass through. If you haven't yet faced these tests, you will. Every friend of God goes through trials. How will you handle them?

> Ties to the natural — Is your passion with that which is familiar, or is your passion for God?

> Severe circumstances — Will you trust God to help you be an overcomer through faith?

> Strife with a brother — Will you be willing to take the lowest place?

Courage — Will you fight for the brother
who messed up his own life?

Desire for wealth — Will you walk in
integrity and make it an important part of
your faith?

Waiting for God — Will you be willing to
wait for God's timing?

Abram was passing test after test until Hagar. The Hebrew word for *Hagar* means "ensnaring." The ways of the flesh ensnare us and lead us into folly. Hagar was an Egyptian and thereby a descendant of Ham (Genesis 10:6). From Noah's prophecy, we know that God's plan was for the Messiah to come through Shem and not through the lineage of Ham.

Ishmael seemed like a good idea at the time to Abram. Abram's flesh was having a hard time waiting for the fulfillment of the promise; Sarai had a quicker and easier way. When we've heard from God but continue to substitute God's plan with our own wonderful ideas, programs, and schemes for a simple faith that waits, we end up in confusion and heartache. When we try to fulfill promises or prophecies with our clever strategies, we're acting in the flesh. God's work must not only be free from sin, it must be free from performance. When God makes a promise, he will keep it. The snares of the enemy can actually be our own ideas that are given birth by impatience. That's why it's so important to hear from him each and every day of your life. Then he will lead you in the way that you should move forward.

During God's delays, our flesh gets agitated and rash. *Why isn't God coming through for me? Maybe I misunderstood? Maybe I need to do something?* The delays of God expose our unbelief. It's one thing to believe the promise at first and quite another thing to hold fast in faith when nothing seems to be happening. Waiting teaches us the ways of God as we trust in the dark. We have a little saying in our house, "Never doubt in the dark what you've heard in the light!"

True faith is not in a hurry. Patience will always be the proof of enduring faith (Hebrews 6:12). When we know our divine friend, we can wait on his timing. In time, the foolishness of our ideas will be seen. Hagar was elated over the honor of bearing a son for Abram. But then Sarai, blaming her husband for the mess, became jealous. Her attitude soured toward her servant until Hagar had to flee.

So often when we see the mistake of acting in the flesh, we punish others for our sorrow and shame. But our outbursts of wounded pride only make matters worse. When we are wrong, we must humble ourselves and confess it. God is there to deliver us.

DIVINE ENCOUNTER

> The angel of Yahweh encountered Hagar by a spring in the wilderness, the spring on the way to Shur. (Genesis 16:7)

Hagar is on the way toward Egypt, but God stops her with a divine encounter. The "angel of Yahweh" appeared to her in the wilderness. God will often lead us into a wilderness to meet us there (Hosea 2:14; Romans 5:6). The place where the Lord often encounters us is "by a spring in the wilderness." It's when we feel like we're in the wilderness of our life and without strength that we find the Lord has a spring of his presence waiting there for us. The place of encounter most often occurs when we feel like we're hitting a wall, a place of emptying. Hagar was being hemmed in by her circumstances and by the rejection she felt. It was her road of self-discovery. *Shur* means "wall." Have you ever felt like you were hitting a brick wall and not going anywhere? It's on the road to Shur that God will open up a spring and release his angel.

The angel doesn't call her Abram's wife but Sarai's servant. The angel commands Hagar to return to Sarai and promises that she, too, will have descendants too numerous to count. The angel also gives her some excellent advice: return, submit, and inherit the blessing. She will have to return to Sarai and give birth to her son. God doesn't speak to Abram or Sarai but to Hagar. And I believe that because of Abram's unbelief, we don't hear of God speaking to Abram again for thirteen years. That's quite a price to pay for doubting the promise of God.

Then Hagar is given a prophecy, complete with the name of her son and his destiny. The angel prophesies that his name is to be "Ishmael," which means "God hears or understands." He will be a wild donkey of a man whose lifestyle is in hostility to all his brothers. He will be untamed, undisciplined, wild, and warlike. Ishmael speaks of the old nature, the beast nature, the flesh. He was a "wild Adam," or a wild donkey that needs to be bridled.

By contrast, the ox nature is the new nature, the nature of our Lord Jesus, meek and serving. The ox will work in a yoke, but the wild donkey never comes under the yoke of another. Ishmael becomes the father of the Arabs. Mohammed, the founder of Islam, came from the line of Ishmael. What great damage and bondage results in Abram's decision to make it happen (Galatians 4:22–26).

The angel of the Lord found Hagar by the well of water in the wilderness. And she names this well "Beer Lahai Roi," which means "the well of the living one who sees me!" She recognized that the angel of the Lord was none other than the "Living One" who saw her in her distress. This same God sees you today, right where you are. He knows your distress and your tendency to flee when difficulty comes. In your wilderness, he's there with fresh revelation of who he is. One way of translating this is "the well of Living Sight" or "the well of Revelation."

This encounter at the well reminds us of a later time when Jesus would journey to a well to meet another woman who had a history of running from God. At the well of Sychar, the Living One came and saw into the heart of a woman who needed mercy, and there he speaks life to her. And he introduces her to the "Fountain of Living Water," causing her to drop her water pot and become one herself—a vessel that carried living water back to her village. May the Lord open our eyes to see the well of the Living One who sees us.

LET'S PRAY

I love you, Lord. You are my comforter and strength. Being near you calms my soul and brings life to my spirit. I want to stay close to your heart today. I choose to walk with you in your footsteps of grace. You know all there is to know about me, yet you still love me. I am overwhelmed in your presence. Draw me closer to your heart. Amen.

14

WALK BLAMELESS BEFORE GOD

*When Abram was ninety-nine years old, Yahweh appeared to him
again and said, "I am the God who is more than enough. Live your
life in my presence and be blameless. I will confirm my covenant
between me and you, and I will greatly multiply your descendants."*

GENESIS 17:1–2

THE ALL-SUFFICIENT GOD

Before grace steps in, Abram had to come to the end of himself.
For thirteen years, God did not appear to him. Abram had only a
promise. Has God left you waiting with only a promise? God once
again appeared to his broken servant to reaffirm his oath that the
son of promise will be born. Why must God's people wait so long for

the fulfillment of the promise of God? Why did so many years have to drag on before God came through for Abraham? Before God, the One who is more than enough and the all-sufficient One, we must learn how insufficient we are in ourselves. Not until Abraham's body was as good as dead (Romans 4:19) did God fulfill his word and give him a son. God's sense of timing is related to our character formation. Every delay has a purpose to it. When we give up, God is ready to act (Psalm 107).

God revealed himself to Abram as "God Almighty," "El Shaddai," "the all-sufficient God." The literal Hebrew is "the nurturing God of the breast," "the nourisher," "the sustainer." The name *El Shaddai* is the most frequently used name of God before the giving of the law by Moses. It reveals God as the strengthener and sustainer of his people. "The God of more than enough," "the all-sufficient God" would perhaps be the best way to convey the meaning of the Hebrew. He not only enriches and protects, but he also makes fruitful. To a man ninety-nine years of age, it will take "the God of more than enough" to fulfill the promises God made to him to give him a son.

How would you like to receive a prophetic word that you were to walk before God blameless? How about if God himself appeared to you with this word? Would it shake you? Would it challenge you? Does it seem impossible? This should be our heart standard. This is the mark of the high calling of God in Christ (Philippians 3:12–14).

Remember, it is "El Shaddai," the "God Almighty," who speaks this word. His name is our power, and we've been called by his name. Because he is almighty and lives within us, we can walk blamelessly. We walk blamelessly as we abide in his presence. We rest in the all-sufficient God working in us to do his perfect will each and every day. It takes omnipotence to change the heart of man. Only God is all-sufficient to lead us into voluntary surrender. Unbelief will rise and whisper of our weakness. Doubts will declare our history of failures. Self will speak up and remind us of our short-lived resolutions and broken vows. It is you alone, God Almighty, who can break our hearts and draw us back to yourself to walk blameless before you.

"Live your life in my presence!" This is true freedom. In his presence, we are free from the false self that walks before others. Our eyes are only for him when we are in his presence. This is to have nothing before our hearts but God himself. If I place my expectations upon others, I'm not walking before God. If I place my expectations in things, I'm not walking before God. Whose presence or what presence do you have before you as the object of your heart? Does God entirely fill your today and your future? Faith fills the heart with God, leaving no room for the enemy to come in. "Only God is my Savior, and he will not fail me" (Psalm 62:5).

A blameless heart carries failure to the cross. To be blameless means we have seen our need but see grace as greater than our fall. We carry no sin, for Jesus carried it on our behalf. *Blameless* means being free from the burden of sin. There is no accusation that abides when we walk blameless before him.

TEN BLESSINGS FOR ABRAHAM

Then Abram fell on his face in awe before God, and God said to him, "I establish this my covenant with you: You will become a father of many nations. You will no longer be named Abram because I am changing your name to Abraham, for I have made you a father of many nations. I will make you abundantly fruitful, more than you expect.

I will make nations out of you, and kings will trace
their lineage back to you. Yes, I will establish my eternal
covenant of love between me and you, and it will extend
to your descendants throughout their generations. I will
be your children's God, just as I am your God. I will
give to you and your seed the land to which you have
migrated. The entire land of Canaan will be yours and
your descendants' as an everlasting possession. And I
will be their God forever!"

…God also said to Abraham: "Concerning your wife
Sarai, you are not to call her Sarai anymore, but Sarah,
'My Princess,' will be her name. I will wonderfully bless
her, and I will certainly give you a son through her."…

Then Abraham laughed so hard he fell to the ground,
saying to himself, "How in the world can a hundred-
year-old man become a father? How can my wife Sarah
get pregnant at ninety?"…

God said, "Listen to me. I promise that you and Sarah
will have a son, and you will call him Isaac. I will confirm
my everlasting covenant of love with him and his seed."
(Genesis 17:3–8, 15, 17, 19)

Abram fell on his face, and God spoke. When we acknowledge
our failure and come to God, he will speak to us in grace. Abram's
posture is a picture of his heart being broken before this revelation of God. Abram becomes a worshiper, bowing low before
the presence of God. And in God's grace, he is given the name

"Abraham," "father of many (nations)." A change of name in Scripture is equivalent to a change of heart. It takes a revelation of the all-sufficient God to truly change the heart of a man. His power affects lasting transformation in Abram, and from that day forward, Abraham would be his name. The work of God in Abram's heart helped Abram see himself in the light of God, causing a radical transformation in him.

He will now be a world-changer, a father of many. *Abram* means "exalted father," and *Abraham* means "father of a multitude." If you had a choice of being exalted or being multiplied, which would you choose? Instead of being highly exalted to the highest place, would you choose to be flattened, broken, and multiplied? Everyone likes being exalted, but God's plan is to multiply us. God wants to see himself expressed through Abraham's multiplication, not through Abraham's exaltation. The church today doesn't need more exalted fathers. What we need are fathers who will multiply themselves in their sons. A generational transfer of blessing is in the heart of God and revealed to Abraham. Here are the ten blessings God spoke over Abraham:

1. I will make you abundantly fruitful, more than you expect.

2. I will make nations of you, and kings will trace their lineage back to you.[11]

3. I will establish my eternal covenant between me and you.

4. I will extend to your descendants throughout their generations.

5. I will be your children's God, just as I am your God.

6. I will give to you and your seed the land to which you have migrated.

7. The entire land of Canaan will be yours and your descendants'[12] to possess as your own.

8. I will be their God forever!

9. I will give you a son, Isaac, by this time next year.

10. I will establish my covenant with Isaac.

When God came to Abraham and announced to him that Sarah would bear him a son, he fell before God and laughed over the impossibility. This had never happened before. Sarah was well past childbearing age—she was ninety. How could a ninety-year-old woman and a hundred-year-old man have a child? Parents and unborn child would all be using walkers! It is humorous indeed. Not only would she have a son, but nations and kings would also come from her. Sarai, which means "princess," now has her name changed to "mother of nations," which would make her queen. Her inner character changed from being a favored "princess" to an exalted "mother of many nations."

God prophesied to Abraham the name of his son, Isaac, which means "he laughs." The naming of the child Isaac was to be a reminder of Abraham's laughter—the joining of faith and doubt seen in his laugh. As for Ishmael, God also promised a blessing to come upon him. Ishmael would likewise become a great nation.

This demonstrates that God's blessings from the beginning are not only to Israel but also for all who believe.

Let's Pray

Almighty God, there is nothing you cannot do! Every limitation in my life is broken when you give grace and glory. I receive the blessings of Abraham—blessings of the miraculous, blessings of favor, and blessings which will pass on to my family. You always keep your word and fulfill every promise. I love you today, my Father and my God.

15

Nothing Is Too Extraordinary for God

Yahweh appeared once again to Abraham while he lived by the oak grove of Mamre. During the hottest part of the day, as Abraham sat at his tent door, he looked up and suddenly saw three men standing nearby. As soon as he saw them, he ran from his tent to welcome them. He bowed down to the ground and said, "My Lord, if I have found favor in your sight, don't pass me by. Stay for a while with your servant."

GENESIS 18:1–3

MESSENGERS FROM HEAVEN

Yahweh once again appeared to Abraham, his friend. We see the Lord's kindness as he came to this man over and over again.

At first, God appeared to Abraham as the God of Glory. Then he showed up as the God Most High, Creator of heaven and earth. Later, he came as El Shaddai, the God who is more than enough, and this time he came in the form of a man, a friend.

If the Lord were to come to you, which way would you prefer? Should he come as the God of Glory and terrify you? Or as the God Most High, leaving you uneasy and uncomfortable? What if he were to come to you as a friend and let you wash his feet? Which would be more pleasant for you? Would you prefer for him to sit on his throne and demand that you bow the knee to him in worship? Or would you rather have him sit with you as your friend under a shade tree so that you can refresh his heart?

What sweet intimacy we see in this chapter! Three times in Scripture we are told that God made Abraham his friend. In 2 Chronicles 20:7, we see God as the one who gave the land to his friend, Abraham. In Isaiah 41:8, God called Abraham his beloved friend. And even better, in James 2:23, because Abraham believed, he was called the lover of God.

You, too, have inherited the blessing since you believed. You are now his chosen friend. Friendship with God is the greatest treasure you will have. Cultivate that friendship with extravagant worship. The Lord comes to his covenant friends and shares his heart with them. He comes not only in majestic splendor but also in the familiarity and freedom of a friend.

Abraham was looking for his day of visitation while living at Mamre. He sat at the entrance of his tent gazing, looking, and longing. When he saw the three men coming, he ran to them. He was ready, anticipating, expecting. This friend of God wanted a visitation. One of these men was none other than the Lord Jesus in human form. Abraham discerned that there was something different about these three men,[13] and he ran to bow down before them. Abraham knew it was his day of visitation, so he bowed low in worship before this man.

And after all his unusual experiences, Abraham knew by now that anything could happen. He understood that there might be something new about to happen, and he didn't take any chances but invited the strangers in. He was ready for anything. He was ready for God the Father to show up anytime, anywhere. He begged the Lord saying, "If I have found favor in your sight, don't pass me by." Abraham wanted the divine guest to remain and abide with him. Abraham was not about to miss this opportunity. He wanted the Lord to stay with him.

THE LORD'S SUPPER

Abraham hurried back into the tent and said to Sarah, "Quick, we have guests! Get three measures of fine flour, knead it, and bake some bread." Then Abraham ran to the herd, selected a tender choice calf, and told his servant, "Hurry—prepare this calf for my guests!" Then he brought the meal they had prepared—roasted meat, bread, curds, and milk—and set it before his guests. Abraham stood by them under the tree while they ate. (Genesis 18:6–8)

Abraham served them a rich meal of roasted meat, bread, curds, and milk, three cakes of fine wheat flour baked over embers, and a tender calf[14] with butter and milk. In both Genesis 18 and Matthew 13:33, three measures ("seahs") of fine flour signify the resurrected humanity of Christ, his life in the believer. Your Lord

Jesus is like the finest of flour baked into cakes and served as food both to God and man.

Can you just imagine God coming to have lunch with Abraham and eating Sarah's cooking? God was the first to drink the milk of the promised land long before the children of Israel did. The cakes of bread, the tender calf, the butter, the milk—it all speaks of the riches of the wonderful Son of God, the Christ who satisfies both God and man. In principle, Abram offered all of this as a sacrifice to God.[15]

Whenever we are in fellowship with God, as we commune with him as our friend, we're offering back to him the riches of his life and sacrifice for us. We never really offer our own sacrifice; we only offer back to God the sacrifice of his Son for his enjoyment. God ate the sacrifice Abraham offered to him, and it represented the life of our risen Lord.

Abraham served his guests himself as he stood near them under the tree. Waiting and ready, this giant of the faith became a servant and washed the feet of his guests. What a picture this was. God had come down as a man to spend time with his friend. Jesus dined with his friend in a covenant meal (Revelation 3:20).

The Lord Jesus loves to come incognito into the homes of those he cherishes. If Jesus would come to us in his manifest presence with glory and splendor, we would have no trouble recognizing him. But what if he comes to visit us as a homeless stranger, a wayfaring man hungry and thirsty, as one seeking refreshment from us? We may pass right by him, not recognizing him as the sick one or the prisoner or the foreigner. In whatever disguise he comes to us, we must be ready, treating every human being with respect and compassion (Matthew 25:45).

After the meal, the conversation began. "They asked him,

'Where is your wife Sarah?'" (Genesis 18:9). That question tells us that these were heavenly visitors. Otherwise, how would they have known Abraham was married? And how did they know his wife's name was *Sarah*? And not only that, but her name had always been Sarai. Had they not been heavenly visitors, they would not have known of the name change, which had taken place immediately preceding this event.

What a confirmation to Abraham's heart! The Lord himself came down to Abraham to tell him that Sarah will have a son. It was as though the Lord wanted to hand deliver the birth announcement. And when Sarah overheard this, she laughed to herself just like Abraham did. Yet she denied it out of fear. Fear makes cowards out of us all. It is faith that makes us truthful and confident. Sarah's faith was born at that moment. When she knew Yahweh had discovered her laughter, a godly fear suddenly filled her. While laughing at God, she realized for the first time that God was at work behind the scenes. She no longer laughed in unbelief because now she believed!

It's important to note that Sarah's folly did not remove her from God's purpose for her life. God doesn't give up on us when we fail. He took it all into consideration when he chose us. Even her laughing at him would not change his mind. He was determined to finish what he began in her heart until she saw his glory. We're all like Sarah. At times, we all manipulate prophecy and judge his promises as impossible. However, God is as kind to us as he was with Sarah, and he still includes us in his divine purpose. It's very possible that one year from now you may look back and see what you thought was an impossibility turn into destiny.

Then the Lord made a statement that should sink deep into every faithful heart: "Do you think that there is anything too marvelous for Yahweh?" (v. 14). There is nothing you're facing right now that the Lord is not sufficient for. The Hebrew word used in this verse is literally *marvelous*: "Is anything too marvelous for the Lord?" This same Hebrew word is used as a title of the Lord Jesus in Isaiah 9:6 (*Wonderful*). Nothing is too extraordinary for God. He is wonderful! This question remained unanswered for three thousand years until Jeremiah the prophet responded by saying, "Nothing is too wonderful for you" (Jeremiah 32:17). God delights in doing the thing that is impossible to man. This child would be known as the Lord's provision.

> Sarah's faith embraced the miracle power to conceive even though she was barren and was past the age of childbearing, for the authority of her faith rested in the One who made the promise, and she tapped into his faithfulness. (Hebrews 11:11)

LET'S PRAY

Father, there is nothing impossible to you! I want to have the faith of Sarah that embraced your miracle power. I'm weak and helpless on my own, but where I trust you, my heart soars in faith! Help me today when I face a challenge to believe your promises. I will trust you with all my heart, for you are my loving Father. Amen.

16

THE POWER OF
INTERCESSORY PRAYER

"Should I really hide from Abraham what I intend to do?"

GENESIS 18:17

ABRAHAM THE INTERCESSOR

What was the message that God came to deliver to Abram? It was the announcement of the birth of Isaac and the destruction of Sodom. Isaac must come, and Sodom must go. Every time Christ comes in, sin must go out. He didn't just come to speak judgment over Sodom, but he also came to reaffirm the promise of a son. It's always the manifestation of Christ (Isaac, the son) that will undo and destroy the works of Sodom (1 John 3:8). His mission is always to produce Christ in us and to destroy the "Sodom" in our soul.

As the three men begin to walk off toward Sodom, Abraham follows along with them. Oh, how we want to linger with the Lord when his presence is near. The closer we walk with Jesus, the more of his heart he'll share with us. As he walks along with his friend Abraham, the Lord begins to share his secrets of what he's about to do (Psalm 25:14; John 15:15). The Lord loves to share secrets with us as we walk close to him and pursue him while he is near. As you cultivate your friendship with Jesus, he won't hold back from you.

The Lord describes Abraham as a man who would lead his family and household to follow God's ways. He would be a good father, a good example. The Father saw in Abraham a heart that would be willing to make a generational transfer to his sons.[16] For this reason, God felt moved to share his secrets with the patriarch. "Abraham remained there, as Yahweh paused before Abraham" (Genesis 18:22). The Lord's desire for Abraham was that he would come to know and understand his ways and teach them to his children after him so that they would live righteous lives. So like a friend, the Father shares the process with him. And he tells Abraham that he's on his way to Sodom to see the extent of their sins, to see how evil and grievous they are. And as they stand there face-to-face, the other two men (angels) take off for Sodom.

So what did Abraham do with these divine secrets? Did he tell the Lord how right he was to judge Sodom? No, he took this information and pleaded for the city. He became Sodom's intercessor. Abraham, God's friend, became an intercessor. Abraham approached God. He remained before God and drew near to his divine visitor. He came up close "like a prince" (Job 31:37 NKJV) to look face-to-face before this man from heaven. Abraham devoted himself to being close to God (Jeremiah 30:21). Why did he draw near? To stand in the gap for others. Hearts enlarged by personal communion with God will take in more of his grace for others.

The sinfulness of man challenging the holiness of God was the "outcry" for judgment. Something must be done with this wicked city. Yet even sharing this with Abraham was an indirect invitation for him to intercede. A tumult of emotion filled Abraham's mind. His heart was broken over his brother's son and this wayward city. He had rescued Lot once, and now he began to plead with the Lord to spare him again and to spare the city of Sodom. Abraham knew they deserved judgment, but he could not understand how God would destroy the righteous and the wicked together. Moving in faith, Abraham boldly spoke to God for those facing judgment. This is true intercession.

His lonely prayer for the lost moved God's heart. As the two of them stood there alone overlooking the city, Abraham humbly reasoned with the Lord. Realizing he was only dust and ashes standing before omnipotence, he pleaded, "Isn't your mercy great enough to forgive?" (Genesis 18:24). You might think this would make God angry. No, this is what he wanted. He was waiting for Abraham's plea to come before him. Abraham was not just expressing what was in his heart, but he was also making a plea that he hoped would move God to reconsider.

What if there are fifty righteous? Forty-five? Forty? Thirty? Twenty? Ten? Six times[17] Abraham asked the Lord for mercy. Each time God drew him out. What if Abraham dared asked for only *one* righteous; would God still destroy the city? What a pity he stopped at ten! Although judgment fell from heaven, the mercy of God is higher than the heavens. God stopped when man stopped. God waited for an intercessor and limited himself to the requests of the intercessor (Isaiah 59:16; Ezekiel 23:30–31). When we think we have asked our limit, God would release more resources of mercy if we would only ask.

FOR THE SAKE OF ONE

> "Roam the streets of Jerusalem, search her streets and public squares, and note what you see. See if you can find even one person who pursues justice. If you find even one searching for integrity, I will surely spare Jerusalem!" (Jeremiah 5:1)

God will deliver a city for the sake of one, yes, even one. Sinful people often believe they have exhausted the mercy of God. We're afraid we've overstepped our bounds. Yet the Father's piercing mercy is boundless and higher than the heavens. We can never expect too much from God. This interchange with Abraham warmed God's heart as he heard him crying out for mercy for his nephew and the city. This Old Testament passage is a classic example for us of how intercessory prayer works.

In Genesis 15:2, Abraham said, "Lord Yahweh, what good is your reward if I remain childless?"

In verse eight, Abraham said, "Lord Yahweh, how can I be sure that I can possess this land for myself?"

In Genesis 17:18, Abraham said, "O, that Ishmael might prosper with your blessing."

But in Genesis 18, Abraham is no longer praying self-centered prayers. He reaches out and prays, not only for Lot, but also for all the other righteous people who he thought might be in the city.

In terms of intercessory prayer, this incident is still phase one in Abraham's life. Later, in chapter twenty, God instructs him to pray for the unrighteous. There was a growing development in his life: First, he prayed for himself, and then he interceded for other righteous people. Eventually, he went a step further as he received instruction to pray for someone who was an unbeliever.

God would have spared an entire city if there had been ten righteous in it. Take note, all intercessors! This is a principle of divine government that you can implement in your intercession for the cities of this earth. We must do more than watch the world slide into darkness; we can avert judgment by our prayers. Here's the formula: We know that if there are only ten righteous in a city that God will deliver that city *if* we will but intercede as we come before him. Even though the cry of wickedness is great in our cities today, the Lord is willing to spare them for the sake of the righteous. Our intercession can turn the tide of judgment.

Abraham did not change the mind of God; he demonstrated it. Abraham knew God well. He knew there was a mercy string to pluck in God's heart of compassion. We must never forget this truth. The Lord is waiting for us to call out his mercy so that he might respond in kind.

Let's Pray

Heavenly Father, you are so kind to me. Your mercy extends beyond my sin and failure. Your kindness humbles me and brings me to repentance. No one is as kind and loving as you. Help me to believe it and walk in the love of God each day. Make me an intercessor like Abraham. I will lift up my family and my city before you today. Mercy, Lord, mercy. Amen.

17

Always Look Forward and Trust God

That evening, the two angels came to Sodom while Lot was sitting at the city's gateway. When Lot saw them, he got up to meet them and bowed with his face to the ground. He said, "Please, my lords, come to your servant's house to spend the night."

GENESIS 19:1–2

FIRE AND BRIMSTONE

Genesis 19 opens with Lot sitting at the gate of Sodom, in a seat of authority, and ends with him hiding in a cave. From councilman to caveman. What a difference a day can make! Apparently, Lot had risen to a place of prominence in this wicked place. How vain it is to achieve success in a world system that will someday be destroyed (1 John 2:17). The world was his snare for twenty years as he dwelt in Sodom. He had chosen the city of Sodom over the tents of pilgrimage that Abraham had chosen.

Abraham entertained heavenly visitors in chapter eighteen, and then Lot entertained them in chapter nineteen. Abraham was waiting for his visitation by the trees of Mamre (under the anointing) while Lot sat at the gate of Sodom. Abraham walked with God while Lot walked in the counsel of the ungodly. Abraham stood in the path of God while Lot stood in the path of sinners. Abraham sat and communed with God while Lot sat in the seat of the scornful.[18] Had Lot lost his logic? Abraham's intervention had rescued him once before, and now he needed rescuing again.

The words the angels spoke to Lot were a condemnation of his lifestyle. They would rather dwell in the streets of Sodom than enter the house of a backslider from God. Lot's insistence, however, won them over. And soon the people of Sodom surrounded Lot's house, threatening to break in and rape the men. So Lot offered his virgin daughters to the lusting mob. (Homosexuality was so prevalent in Sodom that his married daughters were still virgins.) As the argument heated up, the angels pulled Lot inside and struck the mob with blindness.

When Lot discovered who these men were and why they were sent, he hurriedly tried to convince his sons-in-law to join them in fleeing the city. Unlike Noah, Lot could not convince his whole family of the severity of the warning. Their wickedness bound them. Refusing to leave, they were destroyed with the others. Even intercession can't save those who are determined to perish.

The angels had to literally drag Lot, his wife, and daughters out of Sodom. And as they fled, Lot begged to stop at Zoar,[19] a small city nearby. Not wanting to be too far from the city of doom, Lot showed his true colors. In essence, he told God what he wanted to do. What foolishness! It was foolish for Lot to pick his resting place when God wanted to take him to the mountaintop. Interestingly enough, the angels hurried Lot, for they couldn't destroy the city until the righteous had escaped. Even Zoar was spared as a city of refuge for Lot. Our God is so merciful. He spared the righteous. The presence of the righteous will fend off the judgments of God (Revelation 7:3; Ezekiel 9:4).

The sun rose that day just like any other, but the storm clouds of judgment had already formed. And the Lord rained down burning sulfur upon the cities of Sodom and Gomorrah. The Life-Giver had become the destroyer. Judgment fell from the skies with smoke, fire, and burning sulfur. The day of wrath had come for those who rejected holiness. "He will rain down upon them judgment for their sins. A scorching wind will be their portion and lot in life" (Psalm 11:6). Never had there been a day like this. Hell rained down from heaven as God's holy wrath was released. On that day, four hundred years after the flood, fire fell from heaven, and God released the vengeance of eternal fire on the ungodly.

Lot's wife looked back at the judgment of the Lord and turned into a pillar of salt. She was entombed right where she stood. The sense of the Hebrew text is that she lingered behind the others while casting fond glances on what she was leaving. As she did, she was caught in the eruption. Even our Lord Jesus referred to this in Luke 12:32. Just as the destruction of Sodom and Gomorrah serve as an example of what happens to the wicked, so by the example of Lot's wife, we see what happens when the righteous turn back from their righteousness.

Lot's wife's disobedience brought her judgment. And her backward gaze showed that she longed for what she had left; she left her heart there. She didn't fall over dead, but she froze and became a pillar, a monument. May we allow this example to cause us to always look forward and never turn back to the past but to trust God for our future.

> "I don't depend on my own strength to accomplish this;
> however I do have one compelling focus: I forget all of
> the past as I fasten my heart to the future instead. I run
> straight for the divine invitation of reaching the heavenly
> goal and gaining the victory-prize through the anointing
> of Jesus." (Philippians 3:13–14)

Jesus made it clear that if the miracles he did in Israel had been seen in Sodom, they would have repented. Because of this, it will be better off for them on the day of judgment than for several of the cities of Galilee (Matthew 11:20–24). It's clear how we should live, knowing that God will one day judge our corrupt world (2 Peter 3:11–15).

Early that morning, the intercessor, Abraham, got up and returned to his "watchtower" (Habakkuk 2:1) to see what would happen to Sodom. From this elevated place, he saw the smoke of judgment rising in the sky like a belching furnace. It was for the sake of Abraham that God delivered Lot from the catastrophe that destroyed the cities of the plain. A similar scene will take place as the smoke of Babylon's destruction goes up forever and ever (Revelation 19:3).

Lot finally left Zoar and went up into the mountains and into a cave. The safest place for Lot would have been to return in repentance to Abraham and to dwell under his anointing. But Lot wasn't wise enough to know what was best. When Lot aligned with Abraham, Abraham's blessing and favor covered him; it spilled over onto Lot. But when Lot broke covenant and severed the alignment, he quickly went deeper into sin and darkness. Lot ends up in a cave committing incest with his daughters.

While dwelling in the cave with his two daughters, the daughters hatched a scheme. They contrived to sleep with their father in order to propagate the family name. Lot had no sons, and the daughters had no husbands. So they got him drunk with wine and slept with him, the oldest one night and the youngest the next. Whatever their pretense, their plan was vile. Having witnessed the judgment of God upon the wicked, they just didn't seem to understand it. How could the fires of lust burn in them after what they had witnessed of Sodom's flames?

Two sons, or grandsons, came from these incestuous conceptions. They named them Moab, "son of the father," and Ammon, "son of the nearest kinsman." The two boys became the fathers of two nations that became determined enemies of God's people. In fact, the heathen god, Molech, was an Ammonite deity. Even so, because of God's wonderous grace, a Moabitess named Ruth (Ruth 1:4), who was a descendant of Lot, married into the family line of Jesus Christ (Matthew 1:3–5). This just goes to show the far-reaching and powerful nature of God's mercy. His mercy is so great that it even included you and me in his family line.

LET'S PRAY

What a wonderful God you are! Father, I love you. Even in judgment you demonstrate mercy. Your mercy triumphs over judgment! I want to be merciful as my Father in heaven is merciful. Keep working in me until mercy overflows. Help me, Lord, to love mercy and justice and to walk humbly with my God. Amen.

18

SOW A SEED FOR YOUR OWN HEALING

One night, God appeared to Abimelech in a dream and said to him, "You're as good as dead, for you have taken into your harem a married woman!"

GENESIS 20:3

A DETOUR, A DREAM, A BABY

Ancient Jewish historians tell us that Abraham left Mamre (the place of the anointing) to go into the country of the Philistines because of the mocking of his neighbors. So once again, Abraham moved his tents and journeyed to Gerar. Abimelech, the king of Gerar, saw Sarah and took her into his household. And

Abraham lied by telling the king she was his sister. But even so, the Lord didn't forsake him.

God came to Abimelech one night in a dream and warned him of the consequences for taking Sarah, Abraham's wife. It makes you wonder how many times God has warned wayward ones about taking another man's wife in adultery. This pagan king heeded the warning, but how many men don't (Job 33:14–18)? We see from this that God not only speaks in dreams to the righteous, but he will also come to the lost and share his heart with them (Proverbs 21:1). Dreams act as powerful avenues into the spirit of man. God will speak to you in dreams if you will listen.

Abimelech pleaded his innocence to God in the dream, for Sarah and Abraham had assured him that she was his sister. Because of his ignorance, God preserved Abimelech from committing adultery with Sarah. God's restraining hand kept this from happening. It's a wonderful thing when God's mercy comes to hinder us from sinning (1 Samuel 25:32–33). And God commanded Abimelech to restore Sarah to her husband and to ask Abraham to pray for him. God called Abraham a prophet who can pray for him and release healing and restoration. This is the true definition of a prophet. Not only one who speaks for God but also one who will intercede and pray for the restoration of men and women to God. There is great power in the prayer of a prophetic intercessor.

God does not need our lies to protect us. Abraham tried to clear himself by telling Abimelech that Sarah was his half-sister. Regardless, Abraham lied because he feared man. Twenty-five years earlier, Abraham had fallen in the same sin. God will bring out the evil in our hearts so we can see ourselves for what we are. Peter could not have believed that he would deny the Lord until circumstances brought out the evil that was there. When we are finally face-to-face with the truth, the Lord is always waiting there to take us up unto himself.

God had closed the womb of every woman in Abimelech's household, including his servants. But by Abraham's intercession, they were all healed. This is amazing considering Abraham's own wife had never given him a child. The very first healing in the Bible was through the prayer of a childless man, Abraham. He had no confidence in himself as he prayed this prayer of faith. He could only pray by the confidence that he had in God. Abraham understood what a miracle this was, for he prayed for the very thing that he had not yet received.

Praying for someone else when you are sick is sowing a seed for your own healing. When God healed Abimelech's household, it was a catalyst for faith for Abraham's household. When we read the last two verses of Genesis 20 with the first two verses of Genesis 21, we see that Isaac's conception occurred as a result of Abraham's prayer for another person with an identical need. Perhaps this is what James meant when he tells us to "pray for one another to be instantly healed" (James 5:16).

Again we see Abraham blessed materially, even in the place of compromise. Abimelech gave him royal gifts of sheep, cattle, servants, and one thousand shekels of silver (twenty-five pounds) to cover his offense against them. They left richer than when they came.

In the restoration of Sarah, we see a picture of the restoration of the church. Sarah was rejuvenated between chapters eighteen and twenty. She was past the age of childbirth in chapter eighteen, but in chapter nineteen, she was so beautiful that a king desired her. Either the king was blind or a miracle happened. This transformation came in one year because of the authority of her faith and the One in whom it rested (Hebrews 11:11). Truth in her inward parts now brought healing and revitalization. Fragments from the Dead Sea scrolls describe Sarah as the most attractive of women at ninety years old.

THE MIRACLE BABY

> Yahweh visited Sarah, just as he said he would, and fulfilled his promise to her. And Sarah conceived and bore Abraham a son in his old age, at the exact time God had promised them. Abraham named his son Isaac, the miracle son, whom Sarah bore him. When Isaac was eight days old, Abraham circumcised him, as God had commanded him. Abraham was one hundred years old when his son Isaac was born. Sarah said, "God has brought me laughter, and everyone who hears about this will laugh with me." And she added, "Who would ever have told Abraham that Sarah would one day nurse children! Even though Abraham is an old man, look—I have given him a son!" (Genesis 21:1–7)

Not one word of God will fall to the ground unfulfilled. He is faithful even when we doubt. Nothing can hinder God when it's time for a miracle. Is anything too hard for the Lord? So often our wise Father waits until boasting turns to prayer. It's when we're without strength that God moves on our behalf (Romans 5:6). He will wait until we are powerless. Then we know that the miracle must be God, for our strength has failed. Oh, how the Lord delights to do this. We must always remember that God is never in a hurry. It's his divine sense of humor to wait until the last moment before midnight.

They named their miracle son Isaac—"laughter."[20] Every time they called their son, his name reminded them of how God pulled it off. And laughter filled their home as they recounted the miracle birth of their son. He would be the joy of all nations, and they would be blessed through him.

When Isaac was eight days old, his father circumcised him, establishing God's covenant with Abraham and his seed. Abraham was one hundred years old when he finally had a son with Sarah. What a wait! It makes our impatience seem petty. Sarah rejoiced over this son of promise. And she prophesied that others would laugh with her when they heard the news. Sarah, a ninety-year-old woman, nursing a child! Funny, isn't it? Wait, servant of the Lord. His Word will come to pass. Like Abraham and Sarah, you'll be so happy that you, too, will laugh.

In time, Isaac was weaned, and his father threw him a great feast to celebrate the occasion. The milk gives way to solid food (Hebrews 5:11–14). Isaac is a type of Christ who was also born in a time of fulfillment (Galatians 4:4). Notice the details of Isaac's birth and how they foreshadow the birth of our Lord Jesus:

- Both were the promised seed (Genesis 17:6; Isaiah 7:14).

- Both were long awaited (Genesis 12:7, 21:1–3; Galatians 4:4).

- Both had mothers who asked questions (Genesis 28:13–14; Luke 1:34–37).

- Both had names signified before birth (Genesis 17:9; Matthew 1:21).

- Both births were miraculous (Genesis 21:2; Matthew 1:18).

- Both were a delight to their father (Genesis 21:3; Matthew 3:17).

LET'S PRAY

Lord Jesus, I need a greater faith. Help me to trust you in every test and in every difficulty. There is nothing impossible with you. You are always faithful to your Word. I want to be one of great faith. Strengthen my heart to trust you today in everything that I face. You are never intimidated, and I want to hide myself in you. I trust you with all my heart. Amen.

19

FIX YOUR HEART
ON ETERNITY

*Sarah noticed the son of Hagar, the Egyptian, was mocking her son
Isaac. So she said to Abraham, "Get rid of this slave woman and
her son. Banish them, for the son of that slave woman must not
become a coheir with my son Isaac!"*
*Abraham was very upset over Sarah's demand, for Ishmael was his
son too. God spoke to Abraham, "Don't be distressed over the slave
woman and her son. And whatever Sarah says to you, do it, for it
will be through Isaac your promise of descendants will be fulfilled.
Rest assured, I will make the son of your slave woman into a
nation too, because he is your son."*
*Abraham rose up early the next morning, bundled up some food and
a skin of water, and strapped them to Hagar's shoulders. Then he
gave her his son and sent them away. So, Hagar and her son Ishmael*

departed and wandered off into the wilderness of Beersheba.
When the water was gone, she grew desperate, so she left her son
under a bush. Then she walked about the distance of a bowshot
and sat down, for she thought, "I can't bear to watch my son die."
As she sat nearby, she broke into tears and sobbed uncontrollably.
And God heard the voice of the boy. The angel of God called out
to Hagar from the heavenly realm and said, "What's the matter,
Hagar? Don't be afraid, for God has heard the voice of your son
crying as he lies there. Get up! Help the boy up and hold him by the
hand, for I will make him into a great nation." Then God opened
her eyes to reveal a well of water. She went over to the well and
filled the skin with water and gave the boy a long, cool drink.
God was with Ishmael as he grew up in the wilderness of Paran.
He became an expert archer, and his mother, Hagar, arranged a
marriage for him with an Egyptian woman.

GENESIS 21:9–21

HAGAR AND ISHMAEL SENT AWAY

Jealousy was a continual battle in the house of Abraham. As Sarah observed Hagar and Ishmael mocking[21] her son, she could stand their ridicule no longer. Paul used the word *harassed* to describe what took place (Galatians 4:29). The counterfeit will always persecute the ordained. Sarah insisted that Abraham expel their servant and her son.

Abraham was grieved over this matter, but God approved of Sarah's plan. God confirmed Isaac as the true heir. And as soon as Isaac comes, Ishmael must go. It's time to cast out the bond-woman and her son. The casting out of Ishmael is a picture of the believer "casting off" the works of the flesh. As Isaac grew (Christ must increase), Ishmael had to leave (the flesh must decrease). As Hagar and Ishmael fled, they wandered into a desert area where there was no apparent water supply. Mocking the purpose of God will take you to a wilderness.

The Hebrew word for *wilderness* literally means "the place of speaking" or "the place of communing." Isn't it interesting that it takes a wilderness for most of us to truly hear what God is saying to us? We hear from God and commune with him in the desert place. If we understood this, we would not be so quick to run from the wilderness experience. For Hagar, this wilderness was a place of wandering. She lost her way. While trying to make her way through her wilderness, she spent her resources. The little "food and a skin of water" quickly ran out. It was only enough to take her deep into her wilderness...deep into the place of hearing the voice of God.

> "Therefore I am now going to allure her; I will lead her
> into the wilderness and speak tenderly to her." (Hosea
> 2:14 NIV)

Wandering itself is designed by God to bring us to the place of desperation and self-emptying. Wandering reveals our weakness, and it's the place where we learn to lean upon our beloved (Song of Songs 8:5). Wandering is worth the trouble if it will bring us to the place of revelation.

As Hagar went into the wilderness the "water in the skin was gone." She ran dry, and her faith ran out. Has life drained your skin of water? Has your trouble brought dryness to your soul? Are you realizing that you set out with less than what you thought and have now come up empty? That's good, for discovery is waiting for you. Our strength is not in what we have but in God alone. God himself must become our endless supply. God is at the end of your bottle of water.

Giving up hope, Hagar "left her son (Ishmael) under a bush" in the desert. She couldn't stand the sight of watching her son die of thirst, so Hagar sat down "a distance of a bowshot" and began to sob with heart-breaking grief. But the wilderness is also a place where God hears. The Lord heard the sound coming out of the wilderness of Beersheba. God heard the cries of Ishmael and his mother and directed them to a source of water, a well. The Lord replaced her empty skin of water with a springing fountain. "God opened her eyes to reveal a well of water." It takes revelation to see the source of the water of life.

Can you see the tenderness of God toward Hagar and her rejected son? God is the God of the outcast. He is the God of the rejected, the abused, and the forgotten. Here was an unfortunate woman caught in the web of Abraham and Sarah's efforts to achieve their destiny when, suddenly, she was very much in the way. But God would not allow them to die in the wilderness; he rescued them and gave them a new life. God heard her intercession for her son.

"Help the boy up and hold him by the hand, for I will make him into a great nation." The nation of Ishmael began in the wilderness of Beersheba. God said, "This is not the end; it's just the beginning." Many of us think that when we go into the wilderness, we're going to die. But it is only the beginning of something new.[22]

THE COVENANT AT BEERSHEBA

Beersheba is the place where God made covenant with Ishmael. And Beersheba is the place where God also made covenant with Abraham, allowing Abraham to settle in the land in peace. The Philistines knew that God was with Abraham and that he had authority to bless others. For through Abraham, God blessed the nations.

Abraham took this opportunity to bring up an issue that was dear to him, the issue of the well. Everywhere Abraham went, he dug a well and built an altar. Abraham fellowshiped with God at the well, and no one was to interfere with this. He pressed his case with Abimelech until he agreed to confirm their treaty with an oath. Abimelech returned the well to the one who dug it, and Abraham gave him seven ewe lambs. And the place was called Beersheba, "the place of seven wells" or "the well of the oath."

Abimelech's servants had taken Abraham's well by force. Now it was a redeemed well. At the cost of seven ewe lambs, Abraham redeemed this well for Isaac. These seven lambs signify the full, complete, and perfect redemption of Jesus Christ that has released "living water" to his redeemed ones. In the midst of a world that lives without a source of living water, we live by a redeemed source. The water we drink as believers is not natural but supernatural, purchased by the blood of the lamb. We drink his water of life and enter into covenant with him forever. With a redeemed well, Abraham entered a period of rest as he dwelt in the land of the Philistines, where he raised Isaac, in peace.

While in Beersheba, Abraham planted a tamarisk tree, a type of willow that often grows near water. The tamarisk tree did not have a landscaping purpose; it represented a statement of faith. Planting the tree shows faith for endurance until the time of fruitfulness (Isaiah 65:22). You and I are like that evergreen tree planted by a source of living water. In this place, Abraham's life with God deepened even more, and he called Father God "The Everlasting God."

Abraham received a new revelation of God: The Everlasting

God (El Olam), God Eternal. Other translations render this "The Ageless One," "The Hidden One," "The Always God," "the One and Only True God" (Psalm 90:2). This is much more than saying he is the eternal God—it is a statement that he is God forever over all of eternity, God over eternal things. Abraham experienced God as the eternal One, the mysterious One (Isaiah 40:28). Abraham now turned his heart and focus to the God of eternity. The things of the earth were growing meaningless to him. God was preparing Abraham to yield his greatest treasure, his son. It's only as we fix our hearts on eternity that we can ever make sacrifices pleasing to God. When we see him as the eternal One, we're able to let go of temporary things. Abraham touched eternal life as he dwelt by the tamarisk tree at the well. This was the true preparation for giving up Isaac. It's time to experience fellowship by the well of eternal life and to sing, "Spring up, O well!" (Numbers 21:17 NIV).

LET'S PRAY

Eternal Father, you have become everything to me. I long to give you all that I am and all that I have. It is yours—dedicated to you forevermore. Eternity has gripped my heart. I no longer want to live for myself, in my own strength. I lay hold of eternal life and receive the blessing you give to me this day. My heart is fixed on you, my Lord and my God! Amen.

20

WILL YOU PASS
THE TESTS OF ABRAHAM?

*"Now I know you are fully dedicated to me, since you did not
withhold your son, your beloved son, from me."*

GENESIS 22:12

ABRAHAM'S GREATEST TEST

After years of communion with God and years of tests and
trials, Abraham endured the test of a lifetime. Would he offer up
his son of promise? What would you have done? Abraham had let
go of his plan for Ishmael, and then God told him to yield up his
precious Isaac. God was testing his loyalty, proving his sincerity,
and refining his faith. Does this ever happen to you? Doesn't God
test your faith and your loyalty to him? Have you ever had to let go

of something that was very dear to you? Has God ever challenged you to let go of your Isaac? We all want the faith of Abraham, but will we pass the tests of Abraham?

Abraham and Isaac enjoyed sweet years of fellowship with El Olam at the well of Beersheba. Life was good. He had his son, lived by the well, planted a tree, and walked with God. Now the Lord came with a new word: "Please take your son, your only son, Isaac, whom I know you dearly love" (Genesis 22:2).

God plunged the knife into Abraham's soul when he heard these words. But God has an absolute claim upon our lives. As our Maker and King, he has the right to demand from us anything that he pleases. Everything we have comes from him, and we only give back to him what has come from his hand (1 Chronicles 29:16). There are times that our God will come and tell us it's time to give back to him what he has loaned us for a season. If we have thanked him for what he has given, then we must thank him when he comes to take it back.

"OFFER HIM UP TO ME"

God tested no other mortal man in the Bible like he tested Abraham. The test was for Abraham to give his most beloved son, Isaac, the one Abraham had waited all his life to have, the son in whom all his hopes and prophetic words found their fulfillment, to God! Would Abraham love God more than his son? There is no greater test to a father than to offer his son as a sacrifice to God. Yet this is God's way of perfecting faith. He promises us a destiny. Then we wait until it is fulfilled. Then he visits us with this question, *Would you let go of this for me?*

One way to translate *test* could be "lift up." This test was an opportunity for Abraham to be lifted up higher in his devotion and in his love for God. Every test is meaningful in that it can be

God's ladder, his escalator to take us higher in the fires of sacrificial love. We all want Abraham's faith, but do we want Abraham's test to perfect our faith?

The heart becomes God's threshing floor as he sifts wheat from chaff. He does so to prove our love and test our devotion—not to destroy us but to refine us. When God proves us in this manner, it is a sign of him dealing intimately with us. He sees what others do not. He sees not only the negative things we are ashamed of, but he also sees the virtues that he is bringing to maturity. Trials are God's vote of confidence on our future. Every test of our faith brings forth the budding qualities of Christ-likeness. Someday you may call a blessing what you once called a burden.

Every word God spoke here is a sword to Abraham's bones. The heart must be probed to the very bottom. "Take your son," not your lambs or doves but your son! Abraham would have given thousands of lambs to preserve his son. "Your only son," or his only son by Sarah. He had cast out Ishmael. Now must he give Isaac too? Isaac, the son of promise, the son of laughter, "whom I know you dearly love," the beloved son of his old age, the son of miracle power.

Can you see God's open heart of love for his Son in this account? Jesus is the only beloved of the Father's heart. He spared not his own Son (Romans 8:32). Can you imagine the emotion of that moment as God's sword goes deep into Abraham's heart? And so, that sword will visit each of us someday. God may not ask us to sacrifice our sons or daughters, but he will test us on what loves we place before him. The love of God is a jealous fire that can have no rivals. There is a place in God where all other loves are like hatred compared to the fire of passion for God burning in our hearts. Until it consumes us, the sword of testing comes to challenge our faith. May we be found faithful on the day of testing. May we see the hands of wisdom and love behind each trial of our faith. In that hour, we must say, *Here I am.*

"EARLY THE NEXT MORNING..."

Abraham had a heart of ready obedience. Abraham debated God over the impending judgment of Sodom and Gomorrah. Yet here, when commanded to sacrifice his son, Abraham remained silent. We see no mention of doubt, fear, or questions, yet we presume he had many. What would Sarah say? What would Isaac say? This man of faith did not delay to obey the word of the Lord. As the sun began to rise, Abraham set out on the longest journey of his life. True faith never stops to look at circumstances and take a poll to see if it is popular to obey God. Faith simply responds to the words from his mouth. Faith acts on the Word, and that word of grace enables us to do his will.

Abraham was to offer his son as a sacrifice. This is the first time in Scripture we see a shadow of God's request for a human sacrifice. God gave Abraham no reasons, only a command. Abraham must offer Isaac to God in place of a lamb. Isaac was the lamb of Abraham. Jesus is the Lamb of God.

"ISAAC AND I WILL GO UP AND WORSHIP AND THEN WE WILL RETURN TO YOU"

After a heartbreaking three-day journey, Abraham saw Mt. Moriah in the distance, the place where the temple of Solomon was built (2 Chronicles 3:1). David also paid a price for Ornan's threshing floor there (2 Samuel 24; 1 Chronicles 21). These two events teach us a lesson about God's ways. The temple of the Lord will always be built at the place of sacrifice. Abraham had to go to Moriah to become the temple of the Lord and the father of all who believe.

The name *Moriah* means "the vision of Yah" or "the vision of Yahweh." Moriah is where you see the Lord and the Lord sees you. Today we have a vision of the Lord on Mt. Zion, which is the church. And there's no cloud there, for we're not in the darkness anymore; we are a people of vision. And Jehovah is seen every time we lay down our Isaacs before him. This mountain represents the place of vision and the place of provision. It's the vision of Jehovah-Jireh, the Lord our provider.

Two young men servants had accompanied Abraham and Isaac to the foot of Mt. Moriah. These two were witnesses and saw the son carrying the wood up the mountain. However, only the father and the son saw what happened on the mountaintop. The serveants were just like the two thieves crucified on Calvary next to Jesus who saw him carry his cross, but they weren't permitted to see what transpired that day between the Father and his Son, the Christ of God.

Abraham carried the fire and the knife. Just like everyone who follows in Christ in faith will carry the fire (passion) and the instrument of death to whatever stands in the way of absolute abandon. Are you carrying the fire and the knife? God the Father carried divine holiness and divine judgment against the sin of man. The beloved Son was "one who was struck down by God and brought low" (Isaiah 53:4).

Abraham described what happened on the mountain as "worship." He did not say he and the lad were going to sacrifice but to *worship*. Faith sees the greatest sacrifice as an act of worship. Sacrifice is what we do, but worship points us to God. Not what we give up but what he receives, this is worship. Worship in spirit and in truth is giving to God the dearest treasure and calling it the delight of worship. Our eyes will not be on what we give up but on him.

LET'S PRAY

Father, all that I am I owe to you. You have watched over my life with the heart of a loving father. You have met my every need and satisfied my soul. I give you access to my affections and desires. I want everything that is within me to bless your name and glorify you. Help me never to hold back when you ask me to surrender all. I trust you today, my strength and my life. Amen.

21

Six Divine Principles of God's Tests

"God himself will provide the lamb for an offering."

GENESIS 22:8

ABRAHAM'S GREATEST TEST

Words often have double meanings. These words tell us that God will provide the lamb, and they make known that the lamb was for "himself." Only God could supply a lamb that would satisfy him. Nothing of man could meet his divine requirements. If a sacrifice for sin must exist, God must supply it. God himself would be the lamb. This is God announcing the gospel to Abraham (Galatians 3:8). There is only one scene in all of human history that surpasses this one.

Abraham bound the guiltless hands of his son to the altar. And he set the wood in order as he prepared to offer Isaac as a burnt offering to Yahweh. His darling son, the heir of promise, the church's hope. Abraham fixed his heart and eyes toward heaven as he tearfully lifted the knife over his son. His act of obedience was a shocking spectacle to men and angels. The voice of the angel of the Lord pierced the sanctity of that moment with a reprieve: "Do not lay a hand on the boy or harm him," he said, "for now, I know you are fully dedicated to me, since you did not withhold your son, your beloved son, from me" (Genesis 22:12).

At just the right time, Abraham turned and saw a ram caught by its horns in a thicket nearby. Abraham's words to Isaac were prophetic; God provided himself a sacrifice! A substitute will one day come and take the place of every son.

God came to Isaac's rescue, and then Abraham realized that it was only a test of his faith. Abraham proved to God that he loved him more than his prophetic destiny. This was proof positive that Abraham was a man of faith. What else could he do to show God that God was first in his life? Grace had triumphed over every passion of his heart. The supernatural bond of faith was greater than the natural bond of human affection. This time God provided a sacrifice in place of Isaac. But at another time on a hill like Moriah, God the Father did not spare his own Son but freely sacrificed him on Calvary's altar. The eternal Father gave us his dearest treasure, his only Son, Jesus.

With a new revelation burning in his heart, Abraham prophesied on Mt. Moriah, and he gave God a new name in this place—YHWH Yir'eh, Jehovah-Jireh! The definition we commonly give for this name is "the Lord will provide." Let it be forever known that on the mountain of the Lord, it will be provided. The secret is to remain on the mountain of the Lord! This mountain represents a certain confidence and place of total helplessness and dependence upon God.

But YHWH Yir'eh means more than this; the most literal Hebrew rendering of this exalted name for God is: "The Lord will appear." One day, he would be seen again on this mountain as the Son being offered. The Lord would appear as the Savior, the substitute. God provides us a ram caught in the thicket of our sins and offers his blood in our place. In this prophetic act of Abraham, he caught the vision on the mountain of a future sacrifice and a future appearance of the Savior of all.

Abraham's obedience led to a fresh revelation of God. How valuable our tests are when they bring us to know our Father. Tests lead us to a new discovery of who he is. Without trials, we're only walking in theory. After a trial, we walk in personal communion with him. As Abraham returned to Beersheba, he walked in the new understanding of God being enough. Do you realize that the "angel of the Lord" that spoke with Abraham was the one who someday would be caught in the thicket of our sins and crucified for us? Jehovah is truly our provider. He provided so great a salvation for us!

Behind the testing of Abraham lies the wisdom of God. Notice these divine principles:

1. When God tests you, what he's requiring of you often makes no sense at the time.

God's command to give up Isaac made no sense at all. As a result, Abraham needed faith. Whenever there's no understanding, we must have faith. God will remove the props of human reasoning to test our heart to see if we will believe his word alone. We must be those who thank him at all times. Loving gratitude must loosen our hold on every cherished thing. You will never lose by giving up anything to God. Faith yields to God even when it doesn't make sense.

2. Faith is never brought to maturity without a measure of suffering attached.

God will someday make you a person of extraordinary faith. Fear will not be a part of your life, for the tests of life will make you confident that God will provide everything. Even Jesus was made perfect through sufferings (Hebrews 2:10; 5:8; Acts 14:22). Faith will carry you through the most severe trials. Faith lives within the veil.

3. We must obey the Holy Spirit even before we know all the details of what is involved.

Abraham's failure in producing an "Ishmael" resulted from his discontent of not knowing all the details of God's promise. God left Abraham hanging…and he leaves you and me hanging too! We must not strike a bargain with God: *Just tell me first where you are taking me, then I'll go.* We must be willing not to know where God is taking us. Obedience is always one moment at a time. Abraham taught us to say, "To obey is better than sacrifice."[23]

4. Others may not understand what God is doing with you.

Abraham left the two servants behind, and he left Sarah behind; only he and God were allowed to see this test. Often God will bring you to the lonely place where others are not allowed to intrude—they wouldn't understand anyway.

5. The most severe test may lie yet in the future.

Abraham had been tested throughout his life. And God proved

him faithful. All of this prepared him for this one final exam. One day, you will face tests to the fullest. Let this confidence be yours just like it was Abraham's—"The Lord will provide!" God will use it to make you into a "living sacrifice" (Romans 12:1).

6. God will not allow us to go on with an unhealthy attachment to our family.

This was an issue in Abraham's life from the very beginning. God told him to leave his father and his nephew behind, but instead, he took them along on his journey. And then we find him wanting a son so badly that he produced Ishmael. But his obedience on Moriah finally put this problem to rest. Many parents view their futures wrapped up in their children instead of in the Lord alone and his plan for their lives. When that's the case, it becomes so easy for us to manipulate their lives to fulfill our own dreams. We must constantly give our children to the Lord until we and they are able to find the blessing of God in the path that he's destined for them to walk in.

So my friend, don't worry if the Lord tests you. It is a sure sign of your promotion.

LET'S PRAY

My loving Father in heaven, your name is to be praised! In every test and trial, I find your grace is enough for me. You have never let go of me, and your love is so strong. I feel it even in my testing. I ask you for more grace as I humble my heart before you. Give me grace to remain strong and pure in every test—with faith that will not waiver. I trust in you, my God and my strength. Amen.

22

One Act of Humble Service

Sarah lived to be one hundred and twenty-seven. She died in the land of Canaan at Kiriath Arba, now known as Hebron. There Abraham mourned and wept for her.

GENESIS 23:1–2

The Death of Sarah

As Sarah passed from this earth at 127 years of age, the bond of love between Abraham and Sarah broke. She died in the land of Canaan where she had lived as a foreigner for over sixty years. And Abraham sincerely lamented and grieved over the passing of his wife, the mother of Isaac. He sat down by her corpse and wept over her and paid tribute to her life of faith with his tears.

The hope of the gospel sets before us a glorious immortality that lives beyond our tombs. In the morning of resurrection, we will see the value of a life of faith. It's clear that Abraham understood resurrection, for he believed that Yahweh had the ability to raise Isaac from the dead. And he had faith that someday Messiah would come and rise from the dead. Abraham purchased a cave in the land of Canaan from the Hittites dwelling in the land. This purchase was an act of faith and anticipation of that resurrection (Matthew 27:52–53). Abraham's intention in purchasing the cave of Machpelah was not only to bury Sarah there but also for his own eventual burial. The word *Machpelah* means "double" or "doubling." It was a double cave. Those buried in this cave would be couples: Abraham and Sarah, Isaac and Rebekah, Jacob and Leah (Genesis 23:19; 25:9; 49:29–32; 50:13). Abraham had a deep and strong faith, faith in the resurrection to come. Death for the patriarchs was a gateway into the resurrection. This cave was more like a bedroom to rest rather than a tomb—more of an altar than a grave. It was an altar to the God of Abraham, Isaac, and Jacob. "God is not God of the dead, but of the living" (Mark 12:27). He is our God!

Isaac was now forty years old, and the culture of the time expected him to marry by the age of thirty. He was long overdue for a wife. And so Abraham wanted to see his son marry before he died. He wanted to have grandchildren; Abraham wanted to see his blessing unite generations. His "seed of promise" would be richly blessed in natural and spiritual wealth, for God had made Abraham rich. And he wanted Isaac to marry a woman from their family line, a wife who would preserve the purity of their lineage. Isaac must marry one of his own kindred, for he saw the Canaanites descending into great wickedness.

So Abraham commissioned the chief servant of his household (Eliezer) to go look for a bride. And with unquestioned loyalty, he set out. Eliezer had been with Abraham from the beginning and was responsible for everything that Abraham owned. Being the trusted servant that he was, it was only appropriate that he was the one sent out. He had the daunting task of crossing the wilderness to find a worthy bride for Isaac.

GIFTS FOR THE BRIDE

"I know he will send his angel before you so that you can find a wife for my son from there."...

So the servant took ten of his master's camels, loaded them with all sorts of gifts, some of the best things his master owned, and journeyed toward the distant land of Mesopotamia until he got to the village where Abraham's brother Nahor had lived. (Genesis 24:7, 10)

This is clearly a picture of the Father releasing the Holy Spirit to seek out a bride for his Son, Jesus Christ. It is the Father, by way of the Holy Spirit (Eliezar), that brings the bride to Jesus as a love gift to the Son (John 17:24). In allegorical form, the details of this chapter point us to the heavenly scene of the gathering of the nations to be the forever bridal-partner for Jesus. For the Holy Spirit is looking throughout the whole earth, gathering together the church, his bride, the wife of the Lamb (Revelation 21:9). And his ministers are friends of the Bridegroom who are sent to awaken bridal love in the nations as they persuade souls to espouse their heart to him (Matthew 9:15; John 3:29; 2 Corinthians 11:2).

Only the trusted servant, the Holy Spirit, is capable of drawing hearts to the Son. He imparts an endless love for him. And the name *Eliezer* means "the God of help" or "the God of endless comfort." Isn't this the job of the Holy Spirit? He is our helper, the Comforter (2 Corinthians 1:3). The Holy Spirit is also under "oath" to bring back a bride to the Lord Jesus! There will be a bride for the heavenly Isaac. And just as Rebekah followed the servant to find her prince, the bride of Christ will willingly follow the Holy Spirit as he leads us to our heavenly Bridegroom. But should Abraham have died before he saw the wedding, the oath still would have been enforced. Under no condition was the servant to take Isaac into the land to search for a bride; the bride had to be willing to come and dwell in the place of promise.

And Abraham prophesied that God's *angel* would go with him in search for Isaac's partner. The success of this mission would depend on divine intervention. Angels would assist in bringing in the bride. The wife of Isaac must be from his own people so the bride of Christ would be of his own family, born from above. For Christ must have an equal yoke partner to share his throne. And she will share all of the Son's dignity, glory, and unity (John 17:22–23). For the seed of Isaac and his bride will bless all the nations of the earth. They will possess everything together.

So Eliezer took ten camels loaded with gifts for the bride. One camel for himself and nine for the bride. The number nine can represent or correspond to the nine *gifts* of the Holy Spirit (1 Corinthians 12:8–10) or the nine fruits of the Holy Spirit (Galatians 5:22–23). The Holy Spirit comes to us bearing gifts for us, the bride. And he decked Rebekah with gold (a picture of the divine nature) and talked with her about Isaac all the way home (Genesis 24:65). This is a picture of the Holy Spirit placing on us the gold of the righteousness of Christ and speaking to us, the bride of our wonderous Prince Jesus (John 16:13–15)!

The servant went to a well of water just outside the city. After a wearying journey he needed to have his camels watered. So he had his camels kneel as he waited by the well to see who would come along. It was "evening" (at the end of the age a bridal company will come forth), and he waited to see who might show up. Then he prayed for the God of Abraham to send the woman God had chosen to be the bride of Isaac. He asked for a very specific sign that would show the true nature of the bride-to-be.

He wondered if she would be willing to water ten thirsty camels from the well. If she were, he would know that she had a true spirit of servanthood. For it would be a lot of work to draw water for these thirsty camels. And she would have to lower her bucket down the well over and over, for one camel can drink twenty gallons—and all this for a stranger! It would probably be dark before she would be able to finish. This would be an exceptional woman to do something like that. And this is what the Lord is looking for in his spiritual bride—one who is willing to serve others.

"Suddenly, before he had finished praying, there was Rebekah approaching the well with her jar on her shoulder" (Genesis 24:15). No sooner did Eliezer pray these things that Rebekah came to draw water from the well. And then, she humbly offered to water all of the servants' camels. She was willing to give to the one in need, the stranger. She was the one, the one who was fit to be the bride of Isaac. She did exactly what Eliezer had prayed. This one act of service qualified Rebekah to be Isaac's bride. This brought her into the lineage of Christ and his inheritance. One act of humble service has the ability to affect the world and bring promotion to our lives (Matthew 10:42).

LET'S PRAY

Father, your plans are perfect! You have led me and guided my life like a Shepherd. You have been so kind and merciful to me. I want to follow your footsteps for the rest of my days. I want to love your plan for my life as much as I love you. Your holy presence goes with me every day of my life, and I am so grateful. Be the King of my heart today, I pray. Amen.

23

SERVING GOD WITH ENTHUSIASM

Abraham's servant hurried over to meet her and said, "Please lower your jar and give me a little drink."… She quickly emptied her jar into the watering trough and ran back to the well to draw more water, until she had watered all the camels.

GENESIS 24:17, 20

Can you imagine this scene? Abraham's servant had only asked for *a little drink,* and she volunteers to water all of his camels. What an extravagant spirit! You know that the bucket had to be heavy. Yet with enthusiasm, Rebekah was willing to serve a stranger at great cost to herself. The Lord will find his most faithful servants in these last days doing menial tasks with joy and hidden from the eyes of others. Are you faithful to God in serving with enthusiasm in the small things? When the true bridal spirit comes upon us, we will love to serve in the same way that Jesus loves to serve.

The name *Rebekah* means "captivating beauty" or "grace that enraptures." She was a beautiful maiden who wasn't afraid to get her hands dirty for God. Like Rebekah, you, too, have a willing spirit that makes you beautiful to him as he adorns you in grace. And just as Rebekah was "a virgin," you have been washed clean before God regardless of what you have been saved from. This must now be your identity.

When Eliezer inquired of others, he found that Rebekah was a near relative to his master (Isaac's second cousin) and that she came from a family of considerable stature. This was going to be a very special marriage, a marriage made in heaven! So he gave her a gold nose ring and two gold bracelets as tokens of love from his master. This was not a payment for services rendered but recognition of the bride-to-be.

Rebekah took Eliezer and his camels home for the night. Eliezer was so moved and so grateful by the invitation that he dropped to his knees in worship. He realized that the God of Abraham had gone before him and had answered his prayer. And so Rebekah ran ahead and prepared the household for their visitor while Eliezer had church.

What energy Rebekah had! After filling over one hundred buckets of water, she now *ran* home to tell her household what had taken place. When Rebekah's brother, Laban, saw her running home with all this gold on he knew that good was upon them (Proverbs 18:16). And he went to find Eliezer to bring him home. Eliezer was still worshiping at the well when Laban came to him and said,

> "Friend, Yahweh has wonderfully blessed you; please, come
> to my home. Why are you standing out here when I have

prepared the house for you and a place for your camels?"
So the man came into the house, and his camels were
unloaded and given straw and feed. (Genesis 24:31–32)

Wouldn't you like the Holy Spirit to *unload* his gifts in your church (house)? Eliezer was so caught up in this moment that he refused to eat until he could explain his purpose in being there. It was the custom of the Middle East to always eat first and talk business later when entertaining guests. But Eliezer was focused on his mission. As a faithful servant, he told them all about Abraham, his wealth, and about his son, Isaac. How the Holy Spirit loves to brag on the magnificence of Jesus! He went on to tell them of the miracle at the well and how God answered his prayer. Then he asked the family to surrender Rebekah to become the bride of Isaac. What suspense! What would Rebekah say? What would her family think about her leaving with a stranger? They said, "This was all planned by Yahweh." So many times we think the events of our life are happenstance, but they may be a divine setup to release the next phase of destiny in our lives.

Rebekah Leaves Her Family to Marry Isaac

"Here stands our Rebekah before you. You may take her
and go and let her marry your master's son and fulfill
Yahweh's plan for her" (Genesis 24:51).

They understood the timing was so supernatural that they couldn't say no to the Lord. And when Abraham's servant heard this, he bowed down in worship and brought out even more gifts for the bride. Gold and silver jewelry, fine clothing, and costly gifts—gifts for the whole family.

The next day, the family begged Eliezer to wait ten more days as they said their farewells to Rebekah. It would be hard to say goodbye to one so loved. But Eliezer pressed his plea to go. Whenever the master tells us to do something, it's never good to delay. Today is the day to say *yes* to God. He didn't want to keep his master waiting that long. Finally, they decided to ask Rebekah what she thought. And she replied, "I will gladly go with him." Among the Hebrews, there can be no valid betrothal unless the bride freely consents. So when Rebekah agreed, the engagement was sealed. They sent her off with her nurse (personal servant) and with this blessing: "Our dear sister, may you become thousands of ten thousands! May your descendants gain possession of the city gates of their foes!" (v. 60).

This was the blessing Rebekah's household prophesied over her and her seed. Destiny was hanging over them that moment as the spirit of prophecy fell. The prophetic blessing was this: The "seed" of Rebekah would receive the same blessing as the "seed" of Abraham—they would possess the gates of their enemies. And the words they used were *gain possession,* not just knock them down. They would take cities! They would possess the places once held by God's enemies.

This is the prophetic promise of a coming anointing that God's people would reach cities. This city-reaching power comes when God's people walk with a "Rebekah spirit." We must become Rebekah's spiritual seed so that we may enter into this anointing. Notice the qualities of this woman and how they line up with the church:

- She was a virgin[24] with a servant-spirit.

- She submitted to her household (church).

- She saw the purpose of God and had an ear for divine things.

- She was willing to leave her family to step into her destiny.

- She was prepared to walk an unknown path with God.

- She was blessed by her household.

- She was willing to follow Eliezer (Holy Spirit).

- She received an abundance of silver (redemption) and gold (holiness).

- She followed Eliezer (Holy Spirit) until she saw Isaac (her bridegroom).

- She covered herself (humility) with a veil before Isaac.

Like Eliezar took Rebekah away, the Holy Spirit carries the bride away and through the wilderness to meet her heavenly Bridegroom. Have you been taken? It's time to be swept off your feet and to see him face-to-face.

Isaac had been dwelling at the well called "Beer Lahai Roi," which means "the Well of the Living One who Sees Me." Father God had indeed seen Isaac and his need for a bride. And wasn't it amazing how the Lord directly lead Eliezer to the bride that he had chosen for Isaac? In the same way, the Father sees the Son's need for a bride and has brought us to the knowledge of his everlasting love for us. As Isaac lifted his eyes, he saw Eliezer bringing Rebekah to be his bride. Both Isaac and Rebekah had the blessing of the Father and their family. Their union would create the extension of the covenant of Abraham on the earth.

When Rebekah saw him, she literally *fell* (translation from Hebrew) off her camel and went to meet him. And in a token of modesty and humility, Rebekah veiled herself as she met her fiancé for the first time. Those who are espoused to Christ must likewise be quick to humble themselves before our King. It was the sight of her bridegroom that brought this response to Rebekah. She did not feel shame or embarrassment. She showed her humility and respect.

The loss of his mother deeply affected Isaac. It had been three years, but he did not find comfort until he met Rebekah. Isaac fell in love with Rebekah. He showed affection as both a son and a husband. Our heavenly Isaac loved his mother too, even on the cross—and oh, how he loved his bride! The joy he longed for was now his.

Let's Pray

Lord Jesus, I love to love you. I love being a part of your holy church, your bride. Every day I drink deeply of your love. The grace you give me sustains me and keeps me strong. I want more grace to be faithful in all that I speak today, all that I do today, and with all whom I meet today. I want to walk with you, close to your heart, each moment of my life. I love you, Lord Jesus. Amen.

24

GENERATIONAL BLESSINGS

Abraham gave all that he possessed to Isaac.

GENESIS 25:5

ABRAHAM AND ISAAC

The blessing of Abraham now comes upon Isaac. Heaven's grace can be passed down from one generation to another. What we do with grace is the issue, but the blessing remains. The Lord once showed me that God's people focus too much on generational curses and ignore the truth of generational blessings. God will bless your family and your generations after you for one thousand generations.[25] Imagine that. Because you have walked in faithfulness and love for God, he will bless your family for one thousand generations. Now that is a promise to claim.

Isaac became a picture of our Lord Jesus, who became the heir of everything (Hebrews 1:2); all of which belonged to Abraham, including all the promises given to him by God. The land would belong to Isaac while Abraham gave other types of gifts to his other sons, both to Ishmael and to the six sons of Keturah. Abraham did this while still living, unlike what we do today, waiting until death to pass on our inheritances. And so Ishmael and the sons of Keturah were sent away to lands distant from Isaac, thus preserving the promise of inheritance to the beloved son of Abraham and Sarah.

Living at least another thirty-five years after the marriage of Isaac and Rebekah, we hear no more about Abraham having any more supernatural experiences or encounters with the Lord. There are always seasons when we walk by faith, without clear visions or dreams to guide us. The Word of the Lord is also in us, not just in our dreams and encounters.

For nearly one hundred years, Abraham and his family lived in Canaan. But the appointed hour came, and he died at 175, a ripe old age. At that time, he was still full of life. He had longed to see a better place but left it all behind for his eternal reward. He finished his course in faith and "joined his ancestors" in the afterlife. Death gathers us to our people. Those who are our people while we live will be our people after we die. His sons, Ishmael and Isaac, buried him as they lay their differences aside in their common sorrow, burying him in the same cave where Sarah was buried.

The Scripture indicates that Isaac received the favor of God after Abraham's passing. Clearly, he had a blessed and anointed life as the son of promise. He walked in the knowledge that God, the Living One, would never leave him. He was born by supernatural power. On Mt. Moriah, he was figuratively raised from the dead, and now he walked into the realm of favor given by the promises of God to his father Abraham.

Isaac was a man of the well. He dug wells and lived near wells of living water.[26] "Isaac settled near the well named the "Well of the Living One Who Watches over Me," which also means "the Well of the Living One who sees me" (Genesis 25:11). This is the same place where Hagar had cried out for deliverance and God heard her. In a time of desperation Ishmael drank from this gracious well. It's the place where God sees our problems and provides flowing waters of mercy and satisfaction. Isaac didn't just visit there; he lived there. He made the all-seeing God his source of supply. He dwelt in the land of the Living One who sees all things. What a great place to live. It was a well of perpetual revelation and grace.

This was also the place where Isaac first met Rebekah. *Beer Lahai Roi* was full of meaning for Isaac. He lived out his life near the presence of God, being filled with living water every day. He knew that the Living One was watching over his life. It doesn't get much better than that.

JACOB AND ESAU

Now, Rebekah was unable to have children, but Isaac pleaded with Yahweh on behalf of his wife because she was barren—and she did get pregnant, for Yahweh responded to Isaac's prayer. During her pregnancy, Rebekah could feel twins thrashing and struggling with each other inside her womb. So she went to inquire of Yahweh, saying, "Why do I have to live with this?" And Yahweh answered her, saying: "The two sons in your womb will become two nations, and the two peoples within you will become rivals. One people will become stronger than the other, and the older will serve the younger." (vv. 21–23)

The struggle and conflict within the womb was quite intense and painful even before they were born. Her two sons were destined to be founders of great tribes. With an ongoing conflict, the eldest would become a servant to the younger. It was by the sovereign choice of God that Jacob was chosen, even though he was the youngest. The youngest was to receive the blessing, and Rebekah, no doubt, remembered this promise in showing favor to Jacob.

Esau and Jacob represented two nations within her womb: self-life and new creation life of the Spirit. These are two types of people that must be separated. "One people will become stronger than the other, and the older will serve the younger." This becomes a principle that the "flesh" must serve the ways of the spirit, for the spirit is stronger (Galatians 5:17). Think about what would happen in the church today if the "older" would serve the "younger?" We must always make a way for the new thing God desires to do and for the new generation that God desires to bless. Eventually, a generational transfer must take place for the church to take the fullness of her inheritance.

The parents knew that the details of their sons' births were prophetic, so they named them accordingly. Esau, the firstborn, was named hairy. The definition of *Esau* is "hairy, shaggy" or "rough." His appearance was more like an animal of the field than a normal baby. And the color of his skin was quite red, so they nicknamed him Edom, which means "reddish." The second child was born grasping the heel of his older brother so they named him Jacob, which means "heel-holder, supplanter" or "to trip up." This is who Jacob was in essence. He struggled for the best starting position as he wanted to be first. He was known for his schemes and the ways that he manipulated others. He was always deceiving to get his own way.

Both sons' names, Esau and Jacob, pointed to their destinies. And God in grace chose the "heel-grabber" to be the carrier of his promise to the nations. God elects to use those the world considers foolish to shame those who think they are wise, and God chose the puny and powerless to shame the high and mighty (1 Corinthians 1:26–27).

LET'S PRAY

Father, I receive the blessing you have for me today. Your blessings cascade over my heart as I walk with you. Today I want to feel and know that I am blessed by my heavenly Father. I want to use the blessings you pour over me to bless others. Bless me so that I might become a blessing to all my family. I want my family to know you and to be blessed by you. I claim your promise that you will bless my family for a thousand generations. I receive it today. Amen.

25

OUR SPIRITUAL BIRTHRIGHT

When the boys grew up, Esau became a rugged outdoorsman and a hardy hunter, but Jacob was more contemplative, content to stay close to home.

GENESIS 25:27

Jacob was a homebody. Esau was an outdoorsman and a skilled hunter. Like Nimrod, Esau was a man of the world who gained advantage through cunning craftiness, not to ignore Jacob's cunning craftiness in other ways. This made quite a household for Isaac and Rebekah. Esau knew how to please his father and won his heart by providing him with wild game to eat. And Jacob knew how to please his mother and simply helped her in the house (tent) wherever he could. Rebekah preferred Jacob, for she remembered the word the Lord had given her concerning him. This coveted birthright had four elements:

1. Until the establishing of the Aaronic priesthood, the one with the birthright would be the head of the family and would exercise the priestly rights.

2. This birthright would be the lineage through which the Messiah would come.

3. The covenant blessings that God gave to Abraham would pass on to the one possessing the birthright (Genesis 12:3).

4. The birthright would assure a double portion of the father's goods (Deuteronomy 21:17).

This highly esteemed position represented one of the highest privileges given by God. Esau was in line to receive it, but he sold the privileges of the birthright as firstborn to his younger brother, Jacob. The price? A good meal. But was that all? According to Jewish tradition, the firstborn had a duty to cook a meal of red stew on a certain day of the year and place it on the grave of Abraham while the firstborn fasted. However, instead of performing this duty, Esau hunted while Jacob took over without Esau's knowledge. Esau's appetite became his master, and his hunger overcame him. He could not wait for another meal and insisted on eating the customary red stew reserved for honoring father Abraham. With unchecked natural desires, Esau had only one thought: to fill his stomach. As a man of the flesh, he lived to gratify his natural desires. To satisfy his cravings, he gave up the honored privileges of the double portion.

This is a very sad picture of what you and I look like when we say *yes* to sin and *no* to God. We forget that we've been crucified to the flesh and our bodies have been given over to the Spirit of God. Everything in us must give way to the increase of Jesus in our inner man. But Esau chose to live without blessing. Esau was like the thief Barabbas who wanted to be set free from the cross. But Jesus would not come down from his cross. We, too, must identify with our Lord and yield our beings totally and completely to his righteous plans for our lives.

Jacob coveted what Esau despised. He had an eye toward the spiritual blessings that would come to the one who the Father blessed. But Esau despised the birthright. He didn't value the treasures of heaven that would be his. He only saw matters of the flesh. Godless Esau is a warning to all who seek to possess their spiritual inheritance (Hebrews 12:16–17). Esau exchanged one morsel of meat, one bowl of soup, for the princely privileges. And later he lived to regret it, through tears and remorse. He could never restore what he gave up. Gratifying our sensual desires has eternal consequences (Philippians 3:17–19).

The aroma of a pot of stew mastered Esau, and the charms of a Philistine girl mastered Samson, just as the question of a maiden mastered Peter. But with Christ and his strength, we can do anything. There is no strength greater than the strength of the Son of God!

None of us will ever really understand human nature. Even when the disciples thought that they had fully yielded to Christ, they couldn't even pray with him for an hour. Believers today read this story of Jacob and Esau and can't understand how Esau could be so consumed with his hunger that he traded his birthright for this red stew. Yet just as easily we trade our privileges in God for the things of this world.

If we could have been there with Esau, we would have put our hand on his shoulder and looked him in the eye with words like: "Are you sure you want to do this Esau? Is it wise to give it all away for a momentary pleasure?" Now is the time to ask the *Esau that lives in you* these same questions. You must treasure and hold dear your spiritual birthrights. You're a child of God, destined to be like Christ. Your birthright is to stand side by side with Jesus Christ in his glory. He has given you the right to be more than a conqueror over all the power of your enemies. You don't have to yield to sin.

Although Jacob was no match for his burly brother in physical strength, he made up for it in his cunning craftiness. His scheme paid off, and Jacob stole the birthright. After the meal, Esau carelessly got up and went away. He didn't even realize what a grave mistake he made. And he made no attempt to revoke the transaction. He had given his birthright to Jacob.

Jacob was a man who learned the discipline of death to the flesh. He faced his fallen nature through all his days until he leaned upon God. Jacob was a fighter from birth. He could deceive anyone, including his own his brother, his father, and his uncle. Jacob had to learn the ways of the Spirit and had to be transformed. In the same way, we must encounter God as the God of Jacob.

The Bible is a mirror that shows us our hearts through the stories of the biblical characters we read about. Many of us are like Esau, willing to sell the blessings of God for momentary pleasure. And many of us are like Jacob, grasping for all we can in this life, even at the expense of submitting to the ways and timing of God.

Let's Pray

My Father, I want to be like you and walk in humility and tenderness to your instruction. Help me to choose your path over my will. You have never failed me nor led me astray. Every time I submit my heart to your ways, blessings pour over me and joy rises up within me. I choose you this day over anything that would take my heart from you. Amen.

26

DRAW FRESH WATER FROM YOUR SPIRITUAL WELL

Now, another famine struck the land, like the one in Abraham's time. Isaac traveled to Gerar where Abimelech was the Philistine king. Yahweh appeared before Isaac and said, "Do not go down to Egypt. Stay in the land that I will reveal to you. Live there as a foreigner, and my presence will be with you. I promise to bless you."

GENESIS 26:1–3

THE BLESSING OF ISAAC

Genesis 26 is the only chapter of the book of Genesis devoted exclusively to Isaac. Isaac was living in Gerar, a Philistine city of Canaan that was under the rule of King Abimelech. There was a famine in the land when Yahweh came. He appeared before Isaac, instructing him to stay in the land and not to go down to Egypt. God would provide for him in the same way that he provides for us in our famine times. And Yahweh reassured Isaac that all the land given to his father would be his. Yahweh renewed the covenant, for destiny must be fulfilled. And he passed down the promises and the blessings he had given to Abraham—and now the blessing comes to Isaac.

So Isaac stayed in the land, but like his father, he lied about his wife and fell into the sin of his father. And he convinced the people living in the land that his wife was his sister. This passage makes it clear that *both* the blessings of the fathers and the sins of the fathers pass on to the next generation. But God rescued Isaac like he did his father from a blunder that would have had major consequences.

It was said of Isaac that he was "the sole heir of all that Abraham had possessed" (Genesis 24:36; 25:5). And as it is with Isaac, it is with us. All the wealth of the Father's house is given to us (Ephesians 1:3)! Since Jesus is the appointed heir of everything (Hebrews 1:2), it can equally be said of us that because we are children of Abraham, then heirs of God himself, and since we are joined with Christ, we also inherit all that he is and all that he has (Romans 8:17).

Isaac's "seed" would unite generations and multiply like the stars of the heavens. And his spiritual seed would be us. Our new birth brings us into God's family, and we now receive everything from our Father. Isaac is a picture of sonship, a son who receives the blessing of his father. And God calls us to be those spiritual sons and daughters who walk in the fullness of our inheritance by faith.

One Hundred-Fold Increase

Isaac planted crops in that land, and in the same year reaped a hundredfold harvest, for Yahweh greatly blessed him! Isaac grew richer and richer until he was extremely wealthy. (Genesis 26:12–13)

God's blessing was upon Isaac, even in the border city of Gerar. He sowed his seed and reaped a bountiful harvest, a hundred-fold blessing from God! Isaac was greatly blessed because he didn't hoard the seed. He sowed on the enemy's land and reaped a great harvest during a time of famine (Deuteronomy 28:1–13; Isaiah 65:13; Psalm 37:19). God loves to bless his people. He will bless you and keep you and make his beautiful face shine upon you.

Isaac reopened ancient wells, and the jealous Philistines filled them back up with dirt. No matter where Isaac dug and no matter how often, the Philistines threw dirt into the wells. And Isaac would open them back up again! Wells speak of our life in the Spirit, a source of refreshing and satisfaction. When there is no satisfaction (no water), it's time to dig deeper. Even in the lowest valley, refreshment waits for those who will dig for it. And once we've opened up a well, we can't allow the enemy to come along and clog up it up again. We must draw fresh water from our spiritual wells every day of our lives.

"One day, when Isaac's servants dug in the valley, they uncovered a spring-fed well" (Genesis 26:19). In Isaac's day, if you dug a well, you became the owner of that well. It wasn't a community source but a private source of supply. There will always be those who get jealous that you have a well and fresh revelation flowing in your life (Matthew 23:13). They want you to be perpetually dependent on them for truth. The word used here for *spring-fed well* can translate to "springing water"—a well to refresh and reveal new truths springing up inside of you.

The Philistines envied Isaac, and they began to quarrel with Isaac over the first and second well he dug. He named the first well *Esek,* which means "strife or argument," and the second well he named *Sitnah,* which means "hostility or contention." But Isaac refused to turn aside, and he moved on to dig a third well which he called *Rehoboth,* which means a "broad place," "enlargement," or "room enough." God's spiritual seed cannot be given to strife and contention. But we must always choose peace over winning an argument.

While living in Beersheba,[27] God dug a well in the soul of Isaac. The strife with others had taken a toll on him. It was time for a fresh encounter with God. When others were jealous and continually harassing faithful Isaac, God visited him. And in this difficult place, Isaac built an altar of worship, pitched his tent, and dug a well. This is a picture of the things that always accompany God's spiritual seed. They build an altar of worship, cultivate the heart of a pilgrim in the earth, and go deep in the refreshing presence of the Lord.

The Lord truly smiled on what Isaac had done in forgiving his enemies, for the same day he made this covenant with Abimelech, his servants brought him the news of a fresh well of water they found. Since Isaac remained silent over the offense of losing wells, God honored him with a new one. And the well of Beersheba became the place of renewed covenant with God and man.

Let's Pray

God, your blessing passes down from one generation to the next. You have promised to bless me for a thousand generations! I pray for my family, and for a thousand generations to experience your wonderful blessings. I delight in your promises today. I will rest in you and find all my strength and comfort in your embrace. I love you, Father! Amen.

27

ISAAC STANDS BY HIS BLESSING

Rebekah picked out the best clothes of her older son Esau, and put them on her younger son Jacob. She covered Jacob's hands and the soft part of his neck with goatskins. Then she handed Jacob the tasty dish and the bread that she had prepared and he took them to Isaac. "Father?" Jacob said. Isaac replied, "Which one of my sons are you?" Jacob answered, "It's I—Esau—your firstborn. I have done as you asked. Please, sit up. Eat some of this delicious game you love so that you may give me your innermost blessing."

GENESIS 27:15–19

Pulling the Wool over Dad's Eyes

How we all want the blessing of our parents! It causes so much strife and jealousy when we feel we have been left out. Jacob, the "heel-grabber," was now after the blessing of the firstborn. For believers today, we have the Firstborn's blessing, for Jesus Christ is the Firstborn of many sons and daughters, and he has poured out blessings innumerable over each one who loves him. You need not strive to receive the blessing you already have. It's important that we walk in the light of these blessings and cherish all that God has given us in Christ.

As death approached, Isaac knew that he must impart the blessing he had received from Abraham. And ignoring the word that Yahweh had given him, saying that the elder would serve the younger, he sought to release this blessing to Esau. But upon overhearing Isaac giving Esau instructions to prepare his meal, Rebekah found Jacob and instructed him to hurriedly fix his father the meal before Esau returned from hunting.

The promise of the Messiah and the land of Canaan was a great trust that was first given to Abraham, passed on to Isaac, and was now ready to be given to Isaac's son. What power there is in a father's blessing. The outcome would change the course of human history. Would Esau receive it or Jacob? It seemed right for the firstborn, Esau, to inherit the blessing. Nevertheless, the Lord used Jacob's trickery to bring upon him the desired blessing. How gracious is God!

This entire episode is a testimony to the conniving nature of man and the overriding purposes of God that our sin cannot thwart. This family was a mess. None of them did what was right or noble in God's sight, yet God's purpose was fulfilled. Isn't that the story of all our lives? We compete for the blessing, trick and deceive others, and choose the flesh over the Spirit because we think that God needs our help to pull it off![28]

And so Isaac's senses, his ability to smell, taste, and feel, deceived him. How often does this happen to you? Have you ever been fooled by what your senses are telling you? It just goes to show that each and every one of us must learn to trust the leading of the Holy Spirit. The Holy Spirit will not lead us astray. We must live our lives crucified to the flesh with its desires.

Jacob lied when he told his father that he was Esau. Then he lied again when his father asked him if he was really Esau. And he lied a third time when he said that God had provided him with the wild game. Sin multiplies in the heart of a deceiver. You tell one lie and that leads to another and then another. Jacob was about to "pull the wool over the eyes" of his father. Jacob went about his scheme and set the meal before his father. And then he patiently waited for the dinner to be over so that he could finally receive the blessing.

How often do we feel like God needs our help? Why do we allow ourselves to think this way? We must totally surrender our lives as crucified to the "Jacob" life, or we'll go through one breaking after the other. Until we recognize that we have been rendered dead unto sin, we'll always resort to our own cleverness to attain the blessing. We'll try to dress ourselves up in our elder brother's garments to receive the blessing. But we're already clothed in our older brother's garments, and we already have his blessing.

What an intriguing picture; Isaac was about to bless Jacob, even though he intended for the blessing to go to Esau. And so, Isaac praised his son, thinking that he was Esau, and bestowed the coveted blessing upon the head of Jacob, the wrong son, and ultimately, God's purpose was fulfilled. Who could search out the mysterious way God carries out his plans (Romans 11:33–36)? What looked like a mistake and a fraud actually fulfilled the purposes of heaven. If it's true in this account, it's true in your life. Every detail of our lives is continually woven together to fit into God's perfect plan (Romans 8:28). Never underestimate the power of God to turn your failures into fruitfulness if you keep loving him.

Isaac blessed Jacob with three things: riches, power, and prevailing grace. The dew of heaven and the fatness of the earth would work together to make him rich. And the power of dominion would be his, especially over his brethren. Prevailing grace would shield him. Curses would come to those who cursed him and blessings to those who blessed him. God would be a friend to all his friends and an enemy to all of Jacob's enemies. Not only do these blessings extend to Jacob, but they are also the blessings of the Father to every spiritual seed of Abraham, Isaac, and Jacob.

Riches, power, and grace also flow out from our Lord Jesus, the Messiah. All of these blessings are his, and he shares them with all of his followers. For the Word says that all the treasures of heaven and earth belong to him. He alone has dominion over the kingdoms of this world. Jesus, the Messiah, our honored King has been blessed by the Father, and woe to those who seek to curse him!

A Blessing Lost, a Blessing Gained

The story continues as Esau finally showed up from his hunting expedition to seek the blessing, but it was too late. Esau's hunting expedition is a picture of the unbeliever in the world. Those who are in the world hunt and search for something to fill their vacuum. They will try anything out in the world to fill the vacancy in their soul when, in reality, that something can only be found in God. It is God himself who fills our vacuum. No man could have been more disappointed in life than Esau. The book of Hebrews describes Esau as a "godless" man. And it was with trembling and bitter tears that he sought the blessing, but it would not be his (Hebrews 12:17).

Esau sold a most cherished possession, his birthright. This was a symbol of dignity and power and was usually a double portion (Genesis 49:3; Deuteronomy 21:17). And being a part of this special family, Abraham's family, it came attached with an extra special spiritual blessing as well. And the spiritual one was even more special than the temporal. The one who carried this blessing would receive the designation of priest of the family or clan. And they would have the privilege of being the depository and communicator of divine secrets. And last but not least, he would have been the link in the line of the descent by which the Messiah would come into the world.

A kiss from his father blessed Jacob but not Esau. All of this caused Esau to hate his brother. Following in the way of Cain, he made an inner vow to murder his brother as soon as his father died. Such is the heart of man. For jealousy can turn to hatred, and hatred to murder. And all because someone else received a blessing that we didn't receive.

Hebrews chapter eleven, the faith chapter of the Bible, gives us a remarkable insight into this account. In Hebrews 11:20, God commends Isaac: "The power of faith prompted Isaac to impart a blessing to his sons, Jacob and Esau, concerning their prophetic destinies." At first glance, it doesn't appear to be an act of faith but a blunder for Isaac to bless Jacob instead of Esau. But God called it faith. What does this mean? Isaac refused to change what he had done. In faith, Isaac blessed Jacob, even though he thought it was Esau, and when he discovered he had been tricked, he stuck to his guns. "Yes, and he will be blessed indeed!" (Genesis 27:33).

Isaac blessed his sons in faith, for he knew the authority that God had given him. And refusing to reverse the blessing was demonstrating even greater faith. It proved that Isaac realized that the spiritual seed could not continue on an earthly level but a spiritual one. Though he didn't deserve it, Isaac let the blessing stand with Jacob. All of this was contrary to Isaac's natural inclination. But instead of doubt or unbelief, he acted by faith. It is the nature of faith to give priority to God's will rather than our own. This is exactly what Abraham had to do with Isaac. Now Isaac had to give up Esau and his opinion of how God was to accomplish his purposes.

When Rebekah heard of Esau's plans, she warned Jacob and sent him away. This would be the last time that she would see her son before she dies. Rebekah hoped that Jacob would remain out of sight long enough for the jealous rage of Esau to subside. Convincing Isaac that it would not be prudent for Jacob to marry a Canaanite woman, they decided to send him to Laban to preserve his life. So Jacob ran away like a refugee. God had Jacob right where he wanted him—alone and afraid.

LET'S PRAY

Father, you have blessed my life beyond measure. My days are filled with your presence and your grace. Each moment I carry the treasures of Jesus Christ within me. I want my life to express your grace and power. I want my life to be filled with Christ, not my striving. I want to rest content with what I have, for I have all things through Christ who strengthens me. Amen.

28

Ascend the Stairway and Find Fulfillment

[Jacob] had a dream of a stairway.

Genesis 28:12

The Stone Pillow

Jacob fled the anger of his brother to hide at his uncle Laban's house in Haran (Syria). But before Jacob left, Isaac once again spoke a blessing over the spiritual seed. He passed on the two great blessings of Abraham: that he would inherit a land of prosperity and father a multitude of generations. At this time, Jacob was probably seventy-seven years old.

Jacob was now alone. You can almost imagine what filled his thoughts as he walked along. Surely he must have considered how wrong it was to deceive his father. He undoubtedly grieved over leaving his mother behind. Perhaps he wondered what kind of reception he would receive from Laban. Whatever his thoughts, Jacob was at the end of himself as he journeyed from Beersheba toward Haran.

Sixty miles from Beersheba, Jacob "encountered a certain place," the place of God's purpose and design (Genesis 28:11). This nothing-out-of-the-ordinary place was Haran, which means "a dry or parched place." Sometimes when you think you're in a dry place, you are really on your way to meet God. Maybe you're at that place right now. God always has *a certain place* to meet with you and to bless you.

The literal translation of the Hebrew text is more dramatic. "And he *collided* with the place!" It was a startling and unexpected encounter. The Hebrew word *Yifgah* suggests a dynamic encounter with an object that is traveling towards oneself. A word in modern Hebrew from the same root is *piguah*, "to hit, blow" or "strike."

Having walked for a number of days, he was weary and exhausted as night fell. In the twilight, he set up camp at Bethel. Jacob took a stone and used it as his pillow. Some believe this was the ancient place where his grandfather, Abraham, erected an altar to Yahweh years before (12:8) and that the stone pillow may at one time have been part of that altar. Jesus is the anointed stone where we must lay our heads. When the anointing of Jesus fills your head (mind), you will see heaven opened and fresh revelation will flow, and you'll begin to perceive the visions of God. In Jacob's helpless, lonely condition, God was about to send a new revelation. With heaven as a canopy above and the cold ground beneath, he rested in the anointing. And he fell asleep, dreamed, saw a vision of the Almighty, and he heard the words of God!

STAIRWAY TO HEAVEN

As Jacob slept on the anointed stone, the heavens opened, and he saw a stairway, a ladder reaching up to heaven. Upon this ladder, ascending and descending, were angels. God himself was at the top of this angel-filled stairway speaking to him. Each rung of the ladder represented a progressive revelation of God's true riches and purpose for our lives found in Jesus Christ. The ladder went both ways, touching heaven and touching earth. God's love goes both ways. He loves his dwelling place, and he loves man made from earth.

Jesus Christ is clearly the ladder that reaches from earth (his human nature) to heaven (his heavenly nature). Jesus spoke to Nathaniel using the analogy of the ladder with angels. He said to Nathaniel, "I prophesy to you eternal truth: From now on you will see an open heaven and gaze upon the Son of Man like a stairway reaching into the sky with the messengers of God climbing up and down upon him!" (John 1:51). Through Jesus, we climb into the heavenly realm and leave this lower life. It's from this realm that we receive spiritual revelation and the Father speaks to our hearts. All of his favors come to us on this Jesus-ladder. Jesus is the only valid entry into the spirit realm. He is the true way into the heavenlies.

The church ladders all fall short, never reaching the sky. But Christ as our ladder reaches all the way into the heavens and bridges all the gaps. His wonderful deeds, his precious blood, and his mighty resurrection have made the reach from earth to heaven. We can now ascend to heaven through our prayer ladder. We ascend and descend with the glory upon us. And our life can also be a "gate" to heaven. For every praying believer can ascend Jacob's ladder and touch the eternal and release it back to the earth.

Jacob's ladder was filled with angels ascending and descending. Who were these angels? Note the order; they ascended first. It doesn't say they were descending and then ascending, which would be true if they were the angels in heaven. If they descended first, they would be leaving heaven to go to earth. But these angels ascended first. They're intercessors, promise-claimers! The Hebrew word translated "angel" is *malak*, which can also be translated "ambassador, messenger, deputy" or "prophet." The Greek word used in the New Testament for angel is *angelos*, or "messenger." So in both Hebrew and Greek, angels can refer to people.

When Paul wrote to the Galatians, he told them they had welcomed him in their midst as if he were an *angel* of God (Galatians 4:14). In Revelation 2–3, John is instructed to write to the seven churches and to the seven "angels" of those churches. Those angels were messengers or pastors over those churches. Even Jesus, in his preincarnate form, appeared in the Old Testament as the angel of the Lord. In Genesis 18:2, three angels, described as three men, come to Abraham (see also 19:1). Angels are also seen as the end-time messengers (Matthew 24:31). God will send his messengers as fiery flames of revival into all the earth. From the ministry of angels (messengers), the great harvest will be brought in. And we are the angelic-ambassadors that ascend and descend upon the Jesus-ladder![29]

Our Lord repeated this revelation to Nathaniel. Nathaniel had his eyes on the earth. He's the one who said, "What good thing could ever come from Nazareth?" But Jesus told him that he would see an open heaven. Listen to the words of St. Germanus of Constantinople[30] as he speaks of "ladder-climbing":

> The souls of Christians are called to assemble with the
> prophets, apostles, and hierarchs in order to recline with

Abraham, Isaac, and Jacob at the mystical banquet of
the kingdom of Christ. Thereby having come into the
unity of faith and communion of the Spirit through the
dispensation of the One who died for us and is sitting at
the right hand of the Father, we are no longer on earth
but standing by the royal Throne of God in heaven,
where Christ is, just as He Himself says: "Righteous
Father, sanctify in Your Name those whom You have for
me, so that where I am, they may be with Me."

End-time intercession must become an ascension up the
Jesus-stairway. We go up to the heavens with our cries for intervention. Then we descend back to earth with the answer. Intercession
is seeing heaven open and the messengers of God ascending and
descending upon the Son of man. Each rung on the ladder represents a progressive revelation of Jesus and our inheritance in him.

It's time for you, his holy angel, to go up. It's time to let your
heart-cry ascend until the promise descends. We must have
answers to our prayers. So it's imperative that we ascend the hill
of the Lord, the Jesus-ladder, the Jesus-stairway. For we all have
equal and direct access in the realm of the Holy Spirit to come
before the Father (Ephesians 2:18). His door is open and the stairway is available to you. But before you can climb, believe you are
his angel and believe that you can ascend. The answers you need
are not on the earth; they are in the throne room. And heaven and
the throne room are closer than you think.

Hello, angel. Did you go to heaven today? Did you go up to
get the will of God for today? Did you bring it back and execute it?
Are you on the stairway today? Climb that Jesus-ladder and find
the fulfillment of your covenant promises, just like Jacob did. God
is saying, *You have to come where I live to get what you need, for*

you have access to the heavenlies. I left the door open and the lights on. Come up, you mighty angels, and praise the Lord for his mighty works. We will find answers to prayers when we ascend with the request and return in faith with the promise fulfilled. This is the secret stairway of the sky (Song of Songs 2:14).

What was God going to tell Jacob? Would he scold him for being a crafty deceiver? Would he rebuke him for his lack of faith? Perhaps God would just strike him dead for all the rotten things he has done. On the contrary. Instead, he revealed himself to Jacob as the one who will never leave or forsake him. This was a revelation of the Father's grace. And a stream of assurance washed over wayward Jacob! For instead of a rebuke, Jacob received a kiss as the Lord renewed the ancient promises with Jacob. He gave him the blessing that Abraham and Isaac possessed. He told Jacob that his descendants would spread out and cover the land like the dust of the earth. And the spiritual seed would continue through Jacob. His descendants would unite generations, multiply, and bless the whole earth! This blessing has passed from one generation to the next. And now, this blessing rests upon you.

LET'S PRAY

> Jesus, you are my stairway to heaven and through you I access heaven's blessings. I love you, King Jesus, my heavenly Lord! I want to ascend the mountain of the Lord and come before you today. I long to be one with you and enter into all that you have for my life. I will gladly go with you wherever you send me, and I will gladly do all that you tell me to do. I am seated with you today in the heavenly realm. I bow my heart before you, my King! Amen.

29

ARE YOU A WANDERER OR A WORSHIPER?

When Jacob awoke from his dream, he said, "Yahweh is here! He
is in this place and I didn't realize it!" Terrified and overwhelmed
he said, "How awesome is this place! I have stumbled right into the
house of God! This place is a portal, the very gate of heaven!"
Early in the morning, Jacob took the stone he had under his head,
set it up as a pillar, and anointed it by pouring oil over the top of it.
He named that place Bethel; though the city was once called Luz.
Then Jacob committed himself to God, saying, "If you will always
be with me and protect me on this long journey, and if you give
me bread to eat and clothing to wear, and if I return safely to my
father's house, then Yahweh, you will be my God! See! I have set up
this sacred stone pillar and it will be your house, God. I promise to
set aside a tenth of all that you give me as my gift to you."

GENESIS 28:16–22

Jacob Awakens and Makes a Vow

As Jacob stirred from his supernatural slumber, he awakened with the exclamation, "Yahweh is here! He is in this place and I didn't realize it!" How many times have we been led to a place where we were not comfortable only to encounter the Lord? Looking back over your life, you have likely said, "Yahweh was there all the time in all that I went through, and I didn't even realize it!" We often meet with God and miss it. He can be an unexpected visitor. There's actually nowhere on earth that he can't visit you. Ordinary places can become holy places.

We were all meant to live under an open heaven and in a realm of unlimited possibility. We were born to live in two worlds. When our eyes are opened, we begin to see the Lord in everything. Heaven will open up before you, and you can access resources for your journey on earth. When Jacob arrived at this place, he was afraid and convinced that he had stumbled into a dreadful place. So it's possible to be in the house of God and not even realize it. But Jacob finally discerned it clearly and rightly called this place *the house of God, the very gate of heaven.*

Only under an open heaven can we truly see the house of God before us. Clarity is revealed between the realm of God's dominion (house) and what is happening on earth. This is actually the first mention of God's house in the Scriptures. God's house is a place filled with his presence, a gateway to heaven, and a stairway with angels. Jacob had great respect for this place of divine encounter. He saw it as the house of the Lord, the residence of divine majesty, the gateway to heaven, where God and man meet. The more we respect God, the more we realize how awesome he is. But if we walk in our old identity and have no respect for God, the house of God is a dreadful place.

The day would one day come when the house of God would be born among us, born of a virgin. Jesus came to be the dwelling place of God and men under one roof, living in one body. Jesus is the God-man, the house of God. As the house, he invites us to dwell in him as one with the Father. And even though Jesus was the initial fulfillment of the house of God, he was not the ultimate fulfillment. Today, the gate to heaven could also be a description of the *church*. We're God's house because the Father dwells among us as his people. And we are the gateway for others to come to God and to be delivered from the power of their sins (John 20:23). What Jacob saw was actually a prophetic picture of the church that would come, a place where angels would ascend and descend.

So a ladder becomes a house that becomes a gate. A gate is a place of transition and access. We walk from one place to get to another through a gate. When we speak of the church being a "gate to heaven," that means everyone on earth should be able to access the reality and resources of heaven through us. Are we an open gate dispensing heaven to our land?

Jesus told Peter (and us) that there are *gates of hell* established by demonic powers that keep people from heaven. So where are those gates of hell? They are in the minds of people, strongholds of darkness that live in our thoughts. For the devil is always empowered by human agreement. And that agreement takes place in our minds. There are gates within us. The gates of hell are destined to be overcome by the house of God, and the gates of heaven are destined to release miracles and majesty to the earth. Our goal must be to agree with heaven at all times so that we become the gate of heaven, the house of God. We're to release heaven freely into every doubt-filled corner of the earth. We've been called to be a gateway people for the free-flow of heavenly realities into our planet.

A Pillow Becomes a Pillar

> Early in the morning Jacob took the stone he had under
> his head, set it up as a pillar and anointed it by pouring
> oil over the top of it. (Genesis 28:18)

Jacob built a memorial to remember this gateway or portal to heaven, using the stone he had placed under his head. The very Christ on whom we rest becomes the house of God for us. Jacob built a pillar from his pillow. This pillar is a picture of the church. For Paul describes the church as a "supporting pillar and firm foundation of the truth" (1 Timothy 3:15). And as he poured oil on the stone, he consecrated it as a memorial to God (Leviticus 8:10–11). As the stairway had its top in heaven, Jacob anointed the top of the pillar with oil.

And just as Jacob used a stone to build the altar, the Father uses living stones to build his house, his people. He places his living stones together and anoints us with oil, the oil of the Holy Spirit. The Father is in the business of transforming us into precious stones, which will make up the celestial city, the New Jerusalem. And he is building this house here and now on the earth. The Father brings heaven to earth as he mingles himself with those who are his.

The anointed stone is Jesus, covered with the oil of the anointing. He is the chief cornerstone. The stone that David threw at Goliath represents him, and he is a picture of the stone that came and conquered kingdoms in Daniel 2. And like Jacob, we can lay our heads upon him and rest.

So Jacob gives this place a new name. It used to be called Luz, which means "separation," but now he calls it Bethel, which means "house of God." In order for us to be the house of God, we separate from the ways of the world. Jacob had to be driven from his world to discover the house of God. We receive revelation when we separate our heart for the Lord in first-love devotion. As we leave the flesh, we enter into his house. This is place that God speaks to us (Hosea 12:4; Psalm 27:4).

Jacob had two things: a heap of stones and a revelation. This is how God begins. What may look like only ruins today (people who feel overwhelmed with problems), God will use to build his house. God is working on that heap of stones to shape and fashion them according to his will. We are his habitation in the Spirit. He is taking us from a heap of stones and fashioning us as he so desires until we are his beautiful dwelling place, his family, the house of God!

The Lord renewed his covenant with Jacob, and it was now time for Jacob to make a vow to God. Jacob vowed to make God his God. But Jacob started out with an if: "If you will always be with me and protect me…and give me bread…and clothing." The "if" here could also mean "Seeing that God will be with me." Jacob furthermore vowed to give back to God a tithe, or a tenth, of all that God gave to him. This is clear proof that he was making a fresh covenant with God. We prove our faithfulness and real commitment by our finances. If you're not committed to God in your finances, you're not committed to God.

And so Jacob was changed from a wanderer to a worshiper. It's time to make an altar of worship out of the place you're in right now. Whether things are going well or you're dwelling in the land of faith for what is to come, it's time to worship him and rename your place Bethel.

Let's Pray

Lord, I know I need to be changed, to be transformed by your presence. So I offer my heart to you today. Change me, O God! Let me see my life the way you see me. Inspire me to keep moving up the "stairway" until I am completely changed. I want more of you in my life. I want to live at Bethel, the house of God. I want to be one who ascends the stairway to heaven. Take me higher into your ways today, in Jesus' name. Amen.

30

ARE YOU PASSIONATE OR LUKEWARM?

*While they were still speaking, Rachel, the shepherdess, drew
near to the well with her father's sheep. As soon as Jacob took one
good look at Rachel, the beautiful daughter of his uncle Laban, he
quickly went over to the mouth of the well and single-handedly
rolled away the stone and watered all the flock of his uncle Laban!
Immediately, he walked up to Rachel and kissed her! Unable to
hold back his tears, Jacob wept aloud. After he composed himself,
he explained to Rachel, "I'm your father's nephew, your aunt
Rebekah's son." Upon hearing this, Rachel ran to tell her father.*

GENESIS 29:9–12

A Kiss and a Cry

As Jacob arrived in Paddan Aram, he saw a well with three flocks of sheep around it. And he asked the men watering their flocks if they knew Laban. At that very moment, Rachel appeared, leading her flock to the well. God had brought Jacob to the very well where his uncle Laban and his daughters, Rachel and Leah, watered their flocks. What a divine appointment!

Jacob's passionate response to seeing Rachel is unrivaled in Scripture. He became superman, rolled the heavy stone away, swept Rachel into his arms, kissed her passionately, and then cried out loud. What an emotional and passionate scene. It only took one look, and Jacob felt instantly drawn to Rachel like a wave to the shore. What was it about her that moved him this way? Was it simply her physical beauty, or was there something more? Ah, that's where the mystery of divine romance is found.

What is it about you that draws Jesus' heart to you over and over again? Our supernatural King, Jesus, is conquered by only "one flash of your eyes" (Song of Songs 4:9). Is it possible that a beauty that you don't even see in yourself irresistibly moves the Son of man? Yes, the Bridegroom King longs for you. For he sees you as his bride and he says, "Let me see your radiant face and hear your sweet voice. How beautiful your eyes of worship and lovely your voice in prayer" (2:14).

Jacob began working for Laban. And after only a month, Laban asked him what he thought his wages should be. And so, because of his intense love for Rachel, Jacob offered to work for seven years in exchange for her hand in marriage. Now that's true love. Seven years! But to Jacob, it seemed but a few days because of the intense love for her. Love can make long, hard service short and easy. This is why Scripture speaks about "how your love motivates you to serve others" (1 Thessalonians 1:3) and "the work you have done for him" (Hebrews 6:10). It's a labor of love. Jacob tended sheep for those seven years in order to get the bride he loved. Jesus has waited seven thousand years for us, his bride that he dearly loves. And like Jacob, he waits and tends his flock like a Shepherd (Isaiah 40:11).

For those seven years, God taught Jacob submission to the rights of the firstborn. In that day and in that culture, it was not right to marry the younger daughter before the *firstborn*. He stole Esau's blessing, and now Jacob would learn by serving Laban another seven years; he learns about the timing of God.

After the seven years, Laban tricked Jacob by giving him the firstborn, Leah, as was the custom of the day. For Laban switched the brides on his wedding night. Leah was weak-eyed and per- haps homely. (Her name means "weary" and "sluggish.") Rachel was lovely, attractive, and winsome. (Her name means "lamb.") He thought that he was marrying Rachel, but the veil that his bride wore fooled Jacob, just as he had fooled his father by wearing hairy skins over his arms so that Isaac thought that he was Esau. When Jacob woke up the next morning in his marriage tent, he found that he had slept with the wrong woman. He had married Leah not Rachel.

THE "LEAH CHURCH" AND THE "RACHEL CHURCH"

When we look at the story of Jacob, Leah, and Rachel as a parable, we will begin to see a picture of a deeper revelation of the church in the last days. There are two types of churches on the earth today coming forth: one with beauty and radiance, ravishing the heart of the Bridegroom and the other one with weak vision and inability to perceive what fully conquers his heart. Of course, only one church of Jesus Christ made up of every believer exists, yet distinctive characteristics set some apart from others within the bride of Christ. Some have a passion that moves God's heart, while others can be lukewarm and distant from the ways of God.

Rachel wasn't a normal girl, for all the other shepherds were men. The fact that she was a shepherdess for her father's flocks shows that she possessed a surrendered heart. This is the Rachel church! In the last days, a bride will exist who is not only beautiful but also not afraid to get her hands dirty as she sees and does what the Father is doing (John 5:19).

Jacob was undone by Rachel. Emotion moved him from the first time he saw her. He ran to her, kissed her, and cried! Something about this girl brought out these actions. No doubt, he saw a partner in her. She shared his DNA as a cousin. He undoubtedly saw himself in her. This is what makes you so attractive to Jesus—you've been made in his image, full of his life, an equal yoke-partner to his heart, and you love him passionately. When he sees you worshiping him at his feet, he can only kiss you and cry.

When Rachel saw Jacob at the well and he kissed her and told her who he was, she ran to tell her father. She ran, not because she was afraid but because she had found the one her heart loved, the one she was looking for. She didn't ask questions about Jacob's background, history, economic status, or career track. She knew he was the one. Everything else would take care of itself.

Rachel was as passionately in love with Jacob as he was with her. Truly, a beautiful love story, a story of love at first sight! Jacob loved her so much that he was willing to work and wait for her until the day when she would become his. This is a picture of the love of Christ for his beautiful Rachel bride.

What was it about Leah that disappointed Jacob? Why couldn't he just be content to marry the oldest sister as their custom dictated? Very little is said of Leah other than "her eyes were weak." Tradition has it that Leah was cross-eyed or perhaps partly blind. She saw things dimly because of her impaired vision. The Leah church does not function with clear vision. She represents those with limited vision who do not discern the timing and ways of God. Like the lukewarm Laodiceans, Jesus instructed this church to buy eye salve so that they could see (Revelation 3:18).

When a church is vision impaired, it will live only by principles, laws, and customs in the Scriptures. It was the custom for Leah to marry Jacob. The Leah church represents those who only relate to Christ through memorizing truths but not releasing their heart and passion to the One who delights in us. But the Christian life is more than faithfulness to the covenants. The real Christian life is receiving the kisses of Christ that release our souls to love him more. So Leah is a type of a legalism found in the church today. She will know the Word of God but not have a clear enough vision to move into a deeper revelation of his love.

Leah, as a picture of the law, could not see clearly, was unloved, and could not perceive the life of the Spirit. And later Leah would have ten sons, which could represent the ten commandments of the law. The fruit of Leah (and her handmaiden or "bondwoman") was only bondage. Jacob had to work after getting her. The works of man are nothing but bondage to the soul. Leah and her sons could not move the heart of Jacob like Rachel and her sons, Joseph and Benjamin. The Leah church will have sons and evangelism, but they will rarely rise higher than simply following principles and the teachings of men with little sense of destiny. They will be married to Jesus but mostly in a logical and practical way.

With weak vision, the Leah church lives in an escapist

mindset, looking for the easy way out—hoping to be taken out of the world instead of having clear vision for taking dominion in this life. The rapture doctrine makes life convenient for escapism. For when there's no strong vision of a last days beautiful, spotless, and victorious bride of Christ, there's not much hope. Escaping from this world fits in well with her weak vision. She's unable to imagine a King who's so ravished with her as his bride that he will partner with her in subduing kingdoms and establishing righteousness on the earth. The Leah church simply can't imagine God raising up a people so full of his glory that they transform nations and reform society.

The Rachel bride can see the passion of her Bridegroom and his glory that will one day cover the whole earth. She has a transcendent vision to believe that all things are possible with this Bridegroom King.

LET'S PRAY

Father, give me eyes to see all that you are doing on earth today! Wash away any discouragement or disillusionment from my eyes until I see your glory. Lord, I want to be yours fully, yielded completely to you. I want my thoughts to be filled with you today and my heart moved by what moves you. Fill me with your Holy Spirit and show me how I can please you today. In Jesus' name, Amen.

31

THE LESSONS OF JACOB AND HIS WIVES

When Yahweh saw that Leah was unloved, he opened her womb, but Rachel remained childless. Leah conceived, gave birth to a son, and named him Reuben, saying, "Because Yahweh looked upon me with compassion in my misery, surely, my husband will love me now!" She conceived again, gave birth to a son, and named him Simeon, saying, "Yahweh has heard that I am despised, and in his mercy, he has given me this son also." Leah conceived the third time, gave birth to a son, and named him Levi, saying, "This time my husband will be joined to me, because now I've given him three sons!" Once again, Leah conceived and gave birth to a son. She named him Judah, saying, "This time I will praise the Lord!" Then she stopped bearing children for a while.

GENESIS 29:31–35

182

LEAH AND RACHEL'S CHILDREN

Leah was the mother of the first four children of Jacob. She was the least loved, but God favored her with children while denying Rachel this blessing. God's ways are not our ways. The Lord was watching over Leah as well as Rachel, and he saw that Leah was not loved. Rachel wanted children but was blessed with her husband's love. Leah wanted Jacob's heart but was given children. There is a mercy-chord in God's heart that is touched by the broken, poor, and unloved. God gives greater honor to the dishonored ones (1 Corinthians 12:24). It is the nature of God to be drawn to those who hurt. God saw her pain, her loneliness, and her heartache. If she only understood how greatly the Lord loved her.

The names Leah gave to her sons were an expression of her desires for her husband. She promised herself that the children she bore would turn his heart toward her. And she felt that if the Lord opened her womb, he would surely open Jacob's heart. Leah's definition of fulfillment would only come through Jacob's love. Envy is often rooted in a struggle to gain identity. With Leah and Rachel, an obvious competition existed to be the one who had Jacob's heart.

Leah called her firstborn Reuben, which means "See! A son!" The Hebrew name Reuben also sounds like the Hebrew for "he has seen my misery." Apparently, the birth of Reuben did not bring Leah any closer to Jacob's heart. And her second son she named Simeon, which means "he hears." This gives testimony to the grace of God in her life. Yet Jacob still loved Rachel more than Leah. So she named her third son Levi,[31] which means "joined," in hopes that Jacob would become emotionally joined to her.

Over the years of struggling with the pain of being unloved, Leah opens her heart to the Lord, and grace touches her. God was tenderly wooing her to himself through the disappointment of her marriage. At last she gives birth to her fourth son and resolves to praise the Lord no matter what. Leah has now become a worshiper of the Almighty and finds her fulfillment in God. So she names her son Judah (praise) and declares, "This time I will praise the Lord!" And this son becomes the father of the tribe of Judah. He is the son from whom Jesus was born after the flesh. Leah, not Rachel, becomes the mother of Judah and ancestor of Jesus. And for us the *Lion of the tribe of Judah* has come, and we, too, can say, "This time I will praise the Lord."

The desire for affection and approval often leads us down depressing paths as we always seek the love of those who reject us. Unrequited love or lack of affirmation is difficult to endure. However, when we pursue love and recognition by any means, we miss the way of faith. The Lord is our identity, not who loves us on earth. No one will ever love us the way Jesus loves us. He must be enough, for his love endures forever. If we're not satisfied with him, jealousy will make us stumble. What would happen to your inner life if today, right now, in your stressful situation, you said, "This time I will praise the Lord!"

There are several lessons we can we learn from this episode with Jacob and his two wives:

1. God works *with* weak people. The Bible often shows us men and women whom God continues to work with and show grace to despite their resistance, failure, and ingratitude. Jesus Christ lived the life we have access to and died the death for all our resistance, failure, and ingratitude. He became the ladder between heaven and earth for us. A strong God became weak so that weak people like us could be saved.

2. God works *through* weak people. God used Laban's trickery to show Jacob his own deceit. This act humbled Jacob, and he began to change. The "Labans" God brings into our lives prove that God is still working in us and will work through us to bring his purposes to pass.

3. God works *in* weak people. In naming her children, Leah uses the personal name for God, *Yahweh*. After looking to her husband for satisfaction after the birth of each son, Leah finally turns to God with the birth of Judah: "This time I will praise the Lord." God chose Leah, the rejected and perhaps homely sister, to carry the messianic seed.

Battle of the Brides

Jealousy filled Rachel as she saw her sister give birth to four sons while she remained childless. With this strange mess of domestic affairs, Rachel ran to Jacob and demanded that he give her a child. And he angrily met her tantrum with indignation, reminding her that only God could give her a baby. It's good to remember that whatever we want, God is the One who holds the key. But instead of going to God, Rachel gave Jacob her maidservant, Bilhah. She gave Bilhah to Jacob so that Bilhah might provide a child for her. The child of this scheme she named Dan, which means "he has vindicated" or "judge." Rachel really believed that God had vindicated her action by giving her this son. It's amazing how easily we can convince our hearts that we are right when we lean on the flesh instead of walking in faith. The mercy of God allowed the birth of Dan, but it did not represent a wholesale vindication of Rachel's deeds. The second child born of Jacob and Bilhah was Naphtali, meaning "obtained by wrestling" or "my struggle." Rachel made a statement by naming him Naphtali. She felt as though she had wrestled the affection of her husband out of Leah's hands by giving him Naphtali. But the wrestling was not over yet.

Leah, refusing to be outdone, gave her maidservant, Zilpah, to Jacob. Now Jacob had four women in his household. And Zilpah bore Jacob a son that Leah named Gad, which means "good fortune" or "a troop comes," indicating that Leah was planning on having more children. Then Zilpah bore a second child, which Leah named Asher, or "happy." Leah knew others would call her happy since she had another son. What a fiasco accompanied the birth of Jacob's children, the twelve tribes of Israel! Out of a dysfunctional home came the beautiful tribes of Israel that bring blessing to the nations. Out of your dysfunctional situation, God may yet give birth to divine purpose. And so, the saga continues.

LET'S PRAY

Lord, I want nothing to hinder your work in my life. Give me eyes to see how wonderful your plan for me really is. I yield my opinions to you today. Not my will but your will be done. I choose the path of love, no matter what I face today. I will love you with all my heart. And I will show your love today to all that I meet. In Jesus' name, Amen.

32

WHAT YOU BEHOLD IS
WHAT YOU'LL CONCEIVE

God listened to Rachel's heart-cry, and had compassion on her, and made her fertile. She conceived, and bore a son, and named him Joseph, saying, "God has taken away my disgrace. May Yahweh add to me another son."

GENESIS 30:22–24

GOD LISTENED TO RACHEL

After seven years of barrenness, the Lord touches Rachel who also finally asks for her own child. And she gives birth to a son, whom she calls Joseph. His name is significant for *Joseph* means "adding" or "he shall add." The name *Joseph* expresses Rachel's desire to have another son. Perhaps Leah's example of praying for a son led Rachel to also seek the Lord for a miracle child. How often in Scripture do we see God waiting until we ask for the miracle?

The sad part of this story is the struggle we see for love and recognition between people chosen by God. To compete for one another's love is to forget the true source of satisfaction and affirmation that is in the Lord alone. He loves us beyond measure. He calls us wonderful, his glorious ones, fulfilling all his desires (Psalm 16:3). Whatever place we find ourselves in life, whether we are being rejected or ignored, oppressed or hated, we must cultivate wholehearted trust in God and find our joy in his love.

After Joseph, the son of Rachel, was born, Leah had no other sons. The law ended with our heavenly Joseph. He fulfilled every commandment. And his name is so significant, "He will add" (another son). There is still another Son who will come from Jacob's seed. It will be the eternal Son, who is still adding many more sons and daughters and bringing them to glory. Here are the names of all of Jacob's sons and a message God wants to give us through them:

> *Reuben* — "See! A Son!" We see the Son of his love, Jesus.

> *Simeon* — "He who hears!" Faith comes by hearing of him.

> *Levi* — "Joined!" When we believe, we are joined to him.

> *Judah* — "Praises!" Jesus puts praises in our hearts.

> *Dan* — "Judgment!" He passed judgment on the works of the flesh.

Naphtali — "Wrestling!" We wrestle with flesh, but he has already won our victory.

Gad — "Good fortune!"[32] Blessings and good fortune flow through him.

Asher — "Happy!" His love has made us happy.

Issachar — "Reward!" He rewards us with answered prayer.

Zebulun — "Dwelling!" Jesus has become our dwelling place.

Joseph — "He will add!" God will add others, for the Father must have a family like him.

Benjamin — "Son of my right hand!" We will sit with him for all eternity at his right hand.

Jacob felt emboldened to approach Laban for permission to leave. He knew that he had to ask him because he understood the importance of spiritual authority. It was the only right thing to do as he would be taking Laban's daughters and grandchildren away from him. At first glance, it seems Laban had a gracious and cordial response to Jacob's request. But in actuality, Laban didn't want to meet with Jacob because he had known through divination that the blessing on his household had come from the favor of God upon Jacob's life. And Laban was selfish. He wanted to keep Jacob around to make himself prosperous.

Jacob and Laban began to argue over the wages Jacob would

receive. It is obvious that these two did not trust each other. Jacob proposed a commission structure that was somewhat tilted in Laban's favor. The arrangement could easily have helped Laban determine whether Jacob cheated him. Jacob's proposal included Laban turning over all of the streaked, speckled, and spotted of his flocks. So Laban removed all the streaked, speckled, and spotted sheep from the flock so that that Jacob could not use selected breeding to cheat him. It was a wonderful idea, but where did Jacob get it? God had appeared to Jacob and showed him the "streaked, speckled, spotted" idea (Genesis 31:10–13). He was acting on a dream from God.

Streaked, speckled, and spotted—this really describes Jacob's soul. Full of ideas that originated in his heart but still not broken before God. There is much that God would do in his servant to make him pure, untainted, and unspotted. For now, these flocks would be a picture of where Jacob was in his walk with the God of Bethel.

God miraculously multiplied the flocks of Jacob. Blessings surround the one whom God favors. And Jacob had a truly unique way of breeding his flocks. It was either a dream or word from God. Jacob mated the animals in front of a watering trough with peeled branches in front of it. And the animals would mate gazing at the peeled branches which somehow caused their offspring to come out streaked, speckled, and spotted. What seemed like magic was really the blessing of God. Through their eye-gate, something supernatural happened so that when the flocks conceived, they brought forth streaked, speckled, and spotted offspring, making Jacob a rich man.

Is there a spiritual lesson for us to learn through this? God wants us to understand that what we see or gaze upon can impregnate us with the object of our vision. You determine what you'll conceive by what you behold. What you put in front of you in a time of spiritual conception is what you'll birth. Are you gazing upon Christ and his kingdom or your need for vindication?

We must set before this generation the true and mighty Christ. By placing the realities of the kingdom God before the open "womb" of this generation, we will begin to see a fruitful harvest of righteousness coming forth. What you gaze upon is what you'll give birth to.

Eventually, Jacob became quite prosperous, owning large flocks, servants, donkeys, and camels. The Lord was with this promise-bearer, for he was the seed that would bring forth the Son in due time. God's grace takes a man and deals with him right where he is. He was in process. God was making him into a prince with God.

LET'S PRAY

Father, I love you! Change my life today. I want to yield to your work in my heart and give you my all. Take everything that is "speckled and spotted" in my soul. Keep cleansing and purifying my heart until I look and live like Christ. I only want you. I ask you to conquer everything in me that wanders from your grace. I am yours! Amen.

33

ASK GOD TO DO IT ALL

Then Yahweh said to Jacob, "Return to the land of your ancestors where you were born; and remember, I will be with you...for I have seen all that Laban is doing to you. I am the God who appeared to you at Bethel, where you anointed a pillar and made a vow to me. Now leave this land at once and return to the land of your birth."

GENESIS 31:3, 12–13

THE GOD OF BETHEL

Jacob had been away from home for twenty years. And he wasn't meant to spend the remainder of his days in his uncle's household. For God had a different purpose for him. When Laban and his sons saw the blessing of God on Jacob, they grew jealous. Even though Laban wanted the blessing, he perceived Jacob as a threat to the family inheritance. They knew that all his wealth had come from their resources. Jacob knew it was time to go because his in-laws were now not as friendly as they once were. God confirmed this to him with the words, "Return to the land of your birth." So Jacob fled from Laban with his wives and flocks without informing Laban.

Note how God came to Jacob with this word: "I am the God who appeared to you at Bethel, where you anointed a pillar and made a vow to me." God reminded Jacob that he was the One who spoke to Jacob in the place where Jacob turned a pillow into a pillar, the anointed altar of devotion. It was time to move on. The winds of divine purpose were blowing on him again. The land of promise was calling. Taking advantage of the three days journey that separated Laban from him, Jacob ran off undetected.

Laban Pursues Jacob

> Laban, along with some of his relatives, took off in pursuit and chased after Jacob for seven days. He had almost caught up with him in the hill country of Gilead, when God appeared to Laban the Aramean in a dream and warned him, "Be careful that you neither harm nor threaten Jacob." (Genesis 31:23–24)

Laban soon found out about his family leaving. So he gathered a considerable force and sets out in pursuit. And on the night before he overtook Jacob's party, God appeared to Laban in a dream and warned him not to abuse Jacob. Clearly, God was with Jacob and was protecting him from the anger of his father-in-law.

A serious dispute ensued, and Jacob protested his innocence to Laban. All the bottled-up bitterness in Jacob's heart came out. And Laban made it clear that only the fear of God's vengeance was restraining him from the use of violence. He even accused Jacob of stealing from him. So Jacob invited him to search their possessions. Obviously, he was unaware that Rachel had hidden the family idols under the saddlebag of her camel and sat on it. And as Laban came to search Rachel's belongings, she protested, saying she was having her menstrual period and couldn't get up. So Laban found nothing.

Before Jacob and Laban parted company, they made a covenant of friendship and protection. And they set up a heap of stones and ate a meal of fellowship together. Laban, the Syrian, gave this heap of stones an Aramaic name. Jacob gave it a Hebrew name. In both Aramaic and Hebrew, the name means "watch post, watchtower, heap (stones) of witness."

Jesus is our "watch post." Ephesians 2:14 states that Jesus made Jew and gentile one, breaking down the middle wall between them. Jacob, a Jew, and Laban, a gentile, found peace at the "watchtower." The heap of stones was to be a witness that would keep them from going past these stones to harm the other. The stones would serve as boundary markers forming a treaty between the two families. And the family of the spiritual seed made their way toward home.

All along the journey home, Jacob's thoughts turned toward his offended brother Esau. Laban was behind him, but a brother who wanted to kill him was ahead. What would Esau do to him? Did he still harbor bitterness toward Jacob? How would Jacob be able to defend himself against the hostility of his brother? God was about to show Jacob, the spiritual seed, the spiritual protection around him.

TWO CAMPS OF ANGELS

> As Jacob continued toward Canaan, the angels of God
> came to meet him! When he saw them, he exclaimed,
> "This is God's military camp!" So he named that place
> Two Camps of Angels. (Genesis 32:1–2)

As Jacob journeyed back to Canaan, the angels of God met
him. Think about what that must have been like. His eyes were
opened to the spirit realm, and the angels of heaven appeared.
The angels encircle us, empower us, and show us how to escape
(Psalm 34:7). They came to welcome Jacob into his inheritance,
Canaan land (Hebrews 1:14). Can you begin to imagine a face-to-
face encounter with two camps of angels? Jacob exclaimed, "This
is God's military camp!" Jacob believed he had stumbled into the
very headquarters of heaven, God's campsite.

Exactly how long Jacob interacted with the angels, we don't
know. He named the place Mahanaim, or "two camps of angels."
Ancient rabbis taught that these two camps of angels gathered
together just to encircle Jacob. One camp was from Mesopotamia
and brought Jacob to the border of Canaan, and the other camp
of angels was from Canaan coming to welcome the patriarch into
the land of promise. The angels danced that day as Jacob neared
his destiny (Song of Songs 6:13). Encircling him, they celebrated
the purposes of God coming to pass with this one who returned
home. The prodigal son had returned!

Mahanaim, like Bethel, was a spot where the heavenly world
made contact with the earth; the invisible realm was opened to the
visible. But what little effect the visitation of angels had upon Jacob.
Once they were gone, his fear of Esau returned. He knew that he
had stolen a birthright and robbed his brother of the blessings of

the inheritance. Jacob began cleverly scheming. He tried to manage Esau instead of leaning on the Lord. He decided to send some servants to inform "his lord Esau" of what had transpired, hoping to find favor. But even though Jacob coached the messengers about what to tell Esau, the messengers came back only to inform Jacob that Esau was on his way with four hundred men.

Now Jacob was "gripped with fear to the point of panic." He was sure he was about to be overrun with 401 men seeking vengeance. So he devised a plan and divided up his people into two camps (borrowing the idea from the angels perhaps). He wanted to ensure that some of his possessions and family would survive. After all, half is better than none, right? This is the human heart, the "Jacob" that lives in each of us. We always have a plan, a clever idea, something that can keep us from having to seek God. No sooner did he stop praying than he resumed the scheming.

There are times when planning will not do; we must pray. To mix planning with praying will divert us from full abandon to God's ways. Our plans will destroy our praying, and our praying will destroy our planning. When we lean on God, we don't lean on our understanding. When our heart is filled with our ideas, we are still managing our lives. The Lord wants to bring us to the place where life is beyond our control. It's time to watch God work as we pray and trust.

For some, prayer is not a voice of faith and dependence but a voice trying to convince God of our ideas. We assume our plans must be the only way God can deliver us. But his ways are not ours. True faith is asking God to do it all. God plus nothing brings deliverance. The only ingredient we add to the mix is obedience to what he tells us to do.

So Jacob prayed. He called out to God, the God of his father

Abraham and the God of his father Isaac. This is God in covenant relationship. Acknowledging his unworthiness compared to the kindness shown him, Jacob took a lowly place before God and asked for divine protection. *I am so unworthy* is always proper when we come to God. We are only worthy because of what he alone has done for us. Humility is the true friend of prayer. Jacob knew that God had provided him with very thing he owned. He had come to Laban with only a staff, but now he was leaving with great wealth. So he reminded the Lord of the covenant promise of a seed and descendants which cannot be counted. Then Jacob prayed, and then he planned again.

He decided that the best plan was to bribe Esau with gifts. This was not faith at work but a strategy to soften Esau's heart and bring reconciliation. He divided up his extravagant presents into three parts with a space between each. And he spread them out to gain the best advantage. How clever! Then he instructed his servants as to what they should say when they brought Esau the gifts. When asked who was sending these flocks and herds, the messengers were to simply say, "They belong to your servant, Jacob. He's sent them as a gift to you." And he sent each group of gifts with the message that Jacob would be coming behind. Jacob was hiding behind his bribes. What an epic performance.

LET'S PRAY

Father God, my days of scheming and striving are over. I rest in you, and I trust your words. Speak to me today. Help me to live in Christ and not in my old ways. You are my true life and my eternal hope. Strengthen me by your Spirit to walk in purity and truth today. Amen.

34

SUBDUE THE JACOB IN YOU

Jacob was left all alone. Suddenly, out of nowhere, a man appeared and wrestled with him until daybreak. When the man saw that he was not winning the match, he struck Jacob's hip and knocked it out of joint, leaving it wrenched as he continued to wrestle with him. Eventually, the man said to him, "Let me go, for the day is breaking." But Jacob refused, "No! Not until you bless me!"

"What is your name?" asked the man.

"Jacob," he replied.

"Not anymore," the man said to him. "Your new name is Israel, for you have struggled both with God and with people and have overcome." Jacob said, "Please, tell me your name."

"Why ask my name?" the man replied, then he spoke a blessing over Jacob.

So Jacob named the place Penuel, saying, "I have seen God face-to-face, yet my life has been spared!"

GENESIS 32:24–30

THE MIDNIGHT WRESTLING MAN

Jacob was alone—all alone and right where God wanted him. To be left alone with God is the only true way of coming to self-discovery. All flesh is like grass before him, planted in dirt, needing to be cut down, and soon to wither. This was the turning point for Jacob. Schemes had failed, and now it was he and God alone.

For God to use a person, that person must first be emptied of self. The Lord met Jacob at a brook named Jabbok. The name of the brook was a prophecy of what God was going to do in his servant. Jabbok means "emptying." We often pray, *Lord, fill us!* But we need to ask the Lord to empty us first.

As far as Jacob knew, God was taking everything away from him—his wealth, his family, and now his clever confidence. How about you? Have you ever visited the brook Jabbok? This was more than a dream, for in the dark of night someone emerged from out of the shadows to deal with the unbroken Jacob. And with his natural eyes, Jacob could discern who it was that emerged from those shadows. He was much like his father, Isaac, when he discerned who deceived him and received his blessing. It was not Jacob wrestling a man but a man who wrestled Jacob. The One that Jacob saw at the top of the stairway in Bethel had come down to wrestle with him. And they rolled together in the mud of Jacob's mistakes.

The midnight wrestling man had come down to drain Jacob of self. In the mud of Jabbok, Jacob finally realized that he was poor, feeble, and clever in himself. Every time we wrestle with someone, there can only be one winner. One will be pinned to the ground, unable to squirm away. Can you picture puny Jacob wrestling with this heavenly man? How silly. Yet how often do we resist the pure and righteous ways of God for our own? Up to this point, we've seen Jacob squirming out of every difficulty. Now he has met the one who is stronger than he. The Jacob in you must be subdued for God's purpose to be fulfilled.

This midnight wrestling man was actually Jesus Christ. He alone knows where to touch us. He touches us in that place of our self-confidence, the hollow of our thigh. And the thigh is the strongest muscle in the human body. The thigh is the place of our natural strength, the place where Jacob must be broken. For the sinews of the old nature must shrivel so that our new nature may come forth in all of its power. This was the goal of that mysterious six-hour wrestling match. The midnight wrestling man will continue to "pin" us until he shatters our love of self. We, like Jacob, must "bite the dust" of our own nature. The Hebrew word for wrestle literally means "to get dusty." The wrestling man forced Jacob to the ground. This was more than an all-night prayer meeting. This was Jacob getting a taste of his dust-nature. Has this midnight wrestler ever come to you? Has he come to you in recent days to reveal your need? Have you felt as if some mighty power were wrestling with you for your own good? Fear not, Jacob's brother or sister, God will finish his work with you as he did with this patriarch.

Jacob didn't know who this man was. He had no clue that he was wrestling with Yahweh himself. The Lord came to uncover Jacob's ways and change his character. Our difficulties must reveal our inner being and show us where we boast, where we are clever, and where we are trying to be self-sufficient. A crisis that is beyond our control is the only way most of us will learn to lean on him. Eventually, we all discover that the one wrestling with us is our friend and our Redeemer!

The prolonged hand-to-hand combat between Jacob and the Lord lasted all night. Then, by one simple touch, Jacob's hip went out of joint. This must have been incredibly painful. The

Father knows just where to touch us. Isaiah was touched on his lips, but with Jacob, it had to be his thigh. With muscles cramping and being unable to see clearly in the dark night, Jacob wrestled an opponent much stronger than himself. Maybe at first Jacob thought that Esau that had come to him? Or maybe he thought this was possibly an enemy sent to harm him. But before the sun rose, Jacob would discover it was the Lord of the covenant he was struggling with.

Jacob grabbed a heel, but God grabbed Jacob's thigh. It's through these private encounters with the Lord that we are transformed and become those whose names have been changed. We are subdued by the power of God (Philippians 3:21). Jacob would enter the land with a limp.

Finally, the strange man said, "Let me go for the day is breaking." But Jacob refused, "No! Not until you bless me!" For Jacob longed for the blessing and would do anything to obtain it. To say this from the heart is the secret of true strength. We borrow from one who has everything to give. Our strength is a borrowed strength. We must become weak before we can become strong. Our clever abilities will never be a pedestal on which to display the power or grace of Christ. Content in weakness, we cling to the source of true power. So even in our miserable situations, we have the power to lay hold of him who has the power to make it a blessing to our soul. The entire book of Job is the Holy Spirit's commentary on this scene in Jacob's history.

Then out of the blue the stranger asked, "What is your name?" What a strange question. Didn't God know his name? By asking this question, God was touching not only Jacob's thigh but also his slumbering conscience. Jacob's memory took him back twenty years earlier to the tent where his blind, aged father had faced him with the same question and he had said, "I'm Esau," and he got away with it. That was twenty years ago, and now the Father of eternity had come to him, insisting that he acknowledge that he was the one who took advantage of his father and his brother. Jacob means "heel-grabber" or "supplanter." The Lord was insisting that Jacob realize the true nature of his heart. By saying his name was Jacob, he confessed his true nature at that time. "I am a deceiver, a cheat, and my name is supplanter." This confession liberated Jacob and opened up the way for inner transformation. Jacob was forgiven.

"Your new name is Israel." Only the Lord has the authority and power to transform us. Jacob was face-to-face with the God of Abraham and his father Isaac. In the gleams of the sunrise, he encountered the light of all life, the light of Israel. His outward limp spoke of God's inward victory and the victorious limp of God's prince, God's Israel. For *Israel* means "prince with God" or "reigning with God." Jacob had held on tight until the blessing came.

Jacob wanted to know the name of the one who conquered him. "Please tell me your name." "Why ask my name?" was his response. We need not ask his name. The conqueror comes in many shapes and forms and can have the name of *husband* or *wife* or *obnoxious coworker.* Our Redeemer will come with different faces to subdue our unbroken hearts. Our real problem is never another person; it is always our natural strength.

Most believers devote their attention to dealing with outward sin, shortcomings, and worldliness of some sort. We fail to realize that the Lord is after our natural strength. The Lord is not only concerned with our outward life but also with our inward, natural life. True transformation comes from the Father's internal touch at the place of our greatest confidence. The places in our heart where we lean into our own wisdom and ability are the places that he goes after. We can try to live without his grace in these areas.

Although the Lord didn't reveal his name, he did impart a blessing, the blessing of transformation. When we're able to admit our need, realizing the truth of our "dust" life, we're finally and truly set free. We're free from pretending. So Jacob named that place *Penuel*, or "the face of God."

Like Jacob, it is often in our most difficult times of wrestling that we come face-to-face with our God and look upon the face of love. Jacob survived that midnight encounter, and as the sun rose upon him, he received the revelation of a new day. Now that he had seen God face-to-face, he could look Esau directly in the eye with confidence and know that the Father was with him.

LET'S PRAY

Lord of glory, I come before you today and ask for grace. Help me to understand your ways and interpret my difficulties properly. I need you, Jesus, to overshadow me with your presence. I want to walk in your footsteps and be pure and holy. As I empty my heart before you today, fill me with all that you are. I love you, my God! In Jesus' name. Amen.

35

Forgiveness Is Sweet to the Soul

When Jacob looked up,
he saw Esau approaching with four hundred men.

Genesis 33:1

Brothers United

Here came Esau with four hundred men while Jacob approached with four women and his children and servants. Jacob divided his children according to their mothers and sent them to Esau one group at a time. And Rachel and Joseph, Jacob's most loved of all, he reserved for last, just in case the anger of Esau broke out against him and his family. He was so clever and put a lot of thought to his strategy, but he was still walking in the wisdom of man. He anticipated vengeance from the hand of Esau, so he exposed those he cared about the least to the first stroke of that vengeance. But Esau's four hundred men were merely attendants to Esau, not an army Esau intended to use to kill them.

Jacob came to Esau limping and bowed seven times (a little overkill) to ensure his gesture of friendship with his estranged brother. Jacob wanted to restore the peace. Respect for others is a good way to start and will always win you favor. The word of the midnight wrestling man rang true, that he would prevail with others.

> But Esau ran to Jacob and hugged him! He threw his arms around Jacob's neck, he kissed him, and they wept in each other's arms. When Esau looked up and saw the women and the children, he said to Jacob, "Who are all these coming behind you?" (Genesis 33:4–5)

How pleasant to be restored to a brother. Imagine the sense of emotional release Jacob (Israel) felt as he stood there hugging Esau. It is good to remember that, in a moment, God can turn enemies into friends. Remember that God turned Saul into Paul! Our hearts must always be postured to reconcile with others who have distanced themselves from us.

As Jacob and Esau wept in each other's arms, the women and children began to appear. First the handmaidens with their children, then Leah with her children, and then, at last, Rachel and Joseph. The discovery of how God had blessed his brother with such a large family stunned Esau and moved his heart. Jacob's oldest child would probably have been about fourteen and the youngest a mere infant. How touching! Uncle Esau was moved deeply.

Jacob spoke of his children as though they were gifts from God, so graciously given to him by God. How we wish every dad would see his children that way and fulfill his God-given role of loving and nurturing his young. Jacob's wives and children all began to pass before Uncle Esau and bowed down before him as Jacob had done. These were all Esau's family too.

Then Jacob said, "Please take the gifts." This actually states in the Hebrew text, "Take the blessing!" The blessing was what Jacob took from Esau, and now he offered blessing back to his brother. This suggests an act of compensation for what he did to Esau twenty years earlier. Excuses were over; Jacob was now making amends. But Esau refused the gifts because he, too, was a man of means and had sufficient supply. God had blessed him with riches too. He didn't need Jacob to pacify him. And so they reconciled, one to the other as brothers.

And once again, Jacob prevailed. He pleaded with Esau to take the gifts. "For truly, seeing your face after all these years, it's like looking upon the face of God! Since you have received me so warmly" (v. 10). For Jacob to say this was remarkable for two reasons. Jacob, transformed into Israel, had just seen the face of God as he spent time in the dust of Jabbok's banks. Now Jacob saw that same glorious face of God through the mending of this relationship with his brother.

Forgiveness is sweet and pleasant to the soul when we are made one again with those we love. It's like gazing on the face of God. We see God most clearly when we touch mercy and forgiveness. Are there some in your life who need to see the face of God in your countenance? Could you show them a side of God they perhaps have never seen before? Could you find it in your heart to forgive even if they were wrong? Every time we encounter an offended brother we see the face of God. The Father won't let it rest. God will deal with us until it's settled. Every time we see their face, we will be reminded of God.

JACOB COMES HOME

Jacob, once the wanderer, began to settle down for a short time. But God's plans for Jacob would not be fulfilled here; he must venture forward. We are too quick to build a temporary shelter for ourselves, only to discover there is more waiting for us ahead.

> Jacob's journey home from Paddan-Aram finally brought
> him safe and sound to the Canaanite city of Shechem,
> where he camped just outside of the city. (v. 18)

Jacob truly came into his inheritance, and the work of God within him made him whole. He was complete and full in the grace of God. The Hebrew phrase can actually mean "Jacob arrived at Shalem, (Jerusalem), the city of Shechem." At last, Jacob entered Canaan and camped near the ancient site of Jerusalem. Interestingly, this was the first place his grandfather, Abram, camped as he entered the promised land. Abraham set out to look for that city; Jacob now camped within sight of it. The work of God had advanced, and the spiritual seed, Jacob, was moving toward the eternal city, Jerusalem!

> He purchased the field where he pitched his tent from
> the clan of Hamor, Shechem's father, for one hundred
> pieces of silver. (v. 19)

Jacob saw a treasure in the field, the place of anointing, the place of *Shalem*. And he purchased that treasure with a hundred-fold obedience (one hundred pieces of silver). Although it was his by the promise of God, he paid the price to own the field. Throughout the Bible, we will see that those who inherit the blessing are those who pay the full price of obedience to God. And in John 4, we have the story of the woman of Samaria, who lived in the vicinity of Sychar or Shechem. That was the piece of land that Jacob bought and gave to his son, Joseph (John 4:5; Joshua 24:32). The well of John 4 was Jacob's well. And it was Jesus who sat on top of the very place where Jacob dwelt at Shechem. Jacob had no clue that his seed would someday sit there. The mighty God of Israel would one day visit Shechem!

There he set up an altar and named it ["El Elohe Israel"]
To the True God, the God of Israel. (Genesis 33:20)

At Shechem, the place of strength, Jacob built an altar to the Lord calling it "To the True God, the God of Israel." He glorified the Lord for the change of his name to Israel. Now God would be the God of Israel. And Jacob dedicated this altar to God. Perhaps the altar erected by his grandfather had fallen down and Jacob merely rebuilt it.

But it's hard to worship God in a place where we're not meant to be. Regardless, this was a milestone in the life of the patriarch. Jacob had now arrived in the land, but he still needed to go farther. He had to return to Bethel to finish building the house of the Lord. God had already revealed himself as the God of Bethel, and this was where Jacob had to go to find the fullness of his destiny and the reality of his blessings!

LET'S PRAY

Lord, so many times I feel like I have fallen short of your plan for my life. Take me further into your heart, into your ways, and into your plan for me. Draw me closer to you, my Lord, so that I experience your constant blessing over my life. I live only for you. I want only you! Amen.

36

TERRIFY YOUR ENEMIES WITH A CLEAN HEART

God said to Jacob, "Arise, go at once to Bethel, and settle there.
Build an altar there to God, who appeared to you when you were
fleeing from your brother Esau."
So Jacob said to his household and to all who were with him, "Get
rid of every foreign god you have, purify yourselves, and change
your clothes. Then come with me; let us go up to Bethel. I will
build an altar there to God who answered my prayer when I was
in distress and whose presence has been with me wherever I have
gone." Then they surrendered all the foreign gods they had as well as
their earrings. Jacob buried them under the oak tree near Shechem.
As they made their way to Bethel, a tremendous fear of God fell
upon all the cities around them, and no one dared pursue them.
Jacob and all the people who were with him arrived in the land of

Canaan at Luz, now known as Bethel. He built an altar there and named it El-Bethel, because it was the place that God had unveiled himself when Jacob was running from his brother.

GENESIS 35:1–7

BACK TO BETHEL   Rom 8-6

God's purpose for Jacob was to lead him to Bethel, the house of God. For it's only from the house of God that we come to understand our destiny (Psalm 27:4). Jacob had vowed to return and build the house of the Lord at Bethel. Now it was time for Jacob to pay his vow and touch the anointed stone. And so God spoke a word that brought conviction and revival to Jacob: "Arise, go at once to Bethel and settle there."

What is it about Bethel that was so important? It was at Bethel thirty years ago that he had met the Lord and gazed into the heavens, seeing the Jesus stairway. As he made the move to Bethel, he would restore first-love devotion. God is looking for a habitation, a dwelling place. The Bible begins with creation but ends with habitation. Progressively, the Creator is preparing to dwell with man. And Bethel is the house of God, his dwelling place.

After Bethel, there was the tabernacle in the wilderness; after that was the Temple of Solomon, and in time, God dwelt with man in the man, Jesus Christ (Isaiah 7:14; John 1:14). Now the church is the dwelling place of God, his living room (1 Corinthians 3:16; Ephesians 2:19–22). Bethel was the beginning, and the New Jerusalem will be the culmination. But first, Jacob had to take the steps of building an altar and dedicating the house of God.

"God…answered my prayer when I was in distress." (Genesis 35:3)

This was a true revival for Jacob. He called for a time of cleansing for everyone in his household. The first thing they had to do was to remove the idols, those that Rachel took years ago when they fled from Laban. When the Lord refreshes his people, we have the desire to clean house and remove the unclean things from our lives. Some of the acceptable idols in the church today could include your education, ambition in the church, ministry, and other desires that replace God. Building an altar must be more important than building a future.

The second thing he told them was "purify yourselves." They needed to bathe themselves in the purity of God. Cleansing the heart is a constant need for all that want endless revival. We must remove every pollutant of the soul (2 Corinthians 7:1). Then Jacob told them to change their clothes. It was time for a new beginning, a fresh start. Our old clothes speak of our old life that we must lay aside as we put on Christ (Isaiah 64:6; Revelation 3:18). And changing our garments signifies changing our manner of life and putting on a new man. All the people obeyed Jacob, forsaking their idols. And to fully bury their past, Jacob buried the idols under the oak at Shechem. Perhaps "their earrings" were idols that they needed to abandon too (Hosea 2:13).

> A tremendous fear of God fell on all the cities around
> them, and no one dared pursue them. (Genesis 35:5)

What was the result of this revival in Jacob's house? As they set out for Bethel, after Jacob and his household removed the idols, cleansed their hearts, and put on new garments, the terror of God fell on entire towns. If God is for us, who could be against us? There was a powerful anointing released when Jacob's people confessed and forsook their sins. Nothing terrifies the enemy like the purification of the saints. Instead of fighting the enemy, we can see them terrified by our clean hearts. It's time to terrify your enemies.

Upon arriving at Bethel, Jacob built an altar and offered sacrifice to God. And he named the altar "El Bethel," which means "God of Bethel" or "The God of the house of God." This was a major turning point in the life of Jacob. He was where he belonged, and he surrendered his life and future into the hands of El Bethel. He was now lost in the purposes of God. Before this, God was called the God of a certain person, for example, the God of Abraham or the God of Isaac. However, in Genesis 35:7, he is the God of the house of God. He was no longer the God of individual people; he was now the God of a corporate body, the house of God.

The New Testament counterpart to Bethel is the church (1 Timothy 3:15). For us, Bethel is not history; it's the church of the living God. We're not just a pile of individual stones, but we're all being built into the house of God. And we must all experience him in such a way that he becomes more to us than just our individual God but the God of the house of God. This is why we come together as a body. We gather together to meet with the God of the house of God. It is time to come to El Bethel.

Jacob's New Name—Israel

> After Jacob returned from Paddan Aram, God appeared to him once again and blessed him, saying, "Your name was once Jacob, but no longer. Your new name is Israel!" (Genesis 35:9–10)

And as Jacob yielded his life afresh to God, burying the past, he received a new revelation of God. The Lord appeared to him and confirmed the change of Jacob's name to Israel. God seemed to be saying, *Didn't I change your name to Israel? Why do you keep calling yourself Jacob? You can no longer call yourself Jacob, for that means you plan to continue living and behaving the way you did in the past. This is your new day! You must show yourself as an overcomer, a prince. See yourself as Israel and live by the revelation of what I've done in you!* God didn't want to multiply Jacob, but he wanted to multiply Israel.

And he revealed his own name as El Shaddai, God Almighty, "the God who is more than enough." Finally, Jacob found God to be more than enough. And so, each one of us must make that discovery too. Every time we yield our heart to Jesus and give him more of our affections, we'll encounter him in a new way.

"Go and have many children and they will multiply." Life comes from God Almighty. Because he is an all-powerful God, his fruit and life can spring up from you and me. The command to be fruitful and multiply is rooted in God's power to make it happen. His almightiness is available to you. You can be fruitful in your walk with him and multiply yourself into many new believers because El Shaddai, the God who is more than enough, is with you. If you will trust him as the God who is more than enough, your life will bear genuine fruit to his glory.

These words to Jacob were a reaffirmation and continuation of God's promise to Abraham, Jacob's grandfather. We see four things that are identical to the promises that God gave to Abraham in Genesis 17:4–6:

- A name change (Abram to Abraham—Jacob to Israel)
- A promise that kings will come from them
- A reference to being fruitful
- A promise that multitudes will come from them
- A promise of a multitude (literally, *congregation*) of nations

The apostle Paul states that Abraham is "the father of us all" (Romans 4:16–17). Abraham and Jacob did not seem to become a father of many nations in the physical sense. So Paul is presenting the possibility that this fruitfulness and multiplication include spiritual children, not just physical descendants. Everyone has a claim to this promise as they come in faith to the incarnation of the spiritual seed, Jesus Christ (Galatians 3:16). Faith, not Jewishness, makes you a child of Abraham, the father of all who *believe*.

"Then God ascended into heaven from the place that he had spoken to him" (Genesis 35:13). What appeared was not an angel. It was the very glory cloud of God's presence. In chapter twenty-eight, Jacob had a dream. But this time it wasn't a dream but a divine encounter. Jacob set up a stone pillar at Bethel and poured a "drink offering" out upon the altar along with oil. Oil and wine were poured out at Bethel![33] This restored his place of fellowship with God. The stone pillar became a picture of the overcoming life, for Jesus promises to make his overcomers *pillars in the house of God* (Revelation 3:12). The blessing makes you a firm, secure fixture in God's presence. Rest in him today, my friend.

LET'S PRAY

Lord Jesus, I want to be near you and focused on you alone today. May my heart be your resting place. Come and find delight in me today as I yield my heart to you. I thank you for the blessing that is upon my life and my family. This blessing will unite the generations and bring my family line into the fullness of your purposes. I give you my heart, and I lift my family up before you today. Bless them all, in Jesus' name. Amen.

37

GOD WILL NEVER DISAPPOINT YOU

From Bethel, they journeyed on, and as they were approaching
Ephrath, Rachel went into very hard and painful labor. As she was
having great difficulty in giving birth, the midwife said to her, "Don't
be afraid, for you're having another son!" With her dying breath,
Rachel said, "His name is Son of My Sorrow," but his father called
him Son of My Right Hand. Rachel died and was buried on the road
to Ephrath (now Bethlehem). Jacob set up a pillar to mark her burial
site, and it is known as The Marker of Rachel's Tomb to this day.

GENESIS 35:16–20

RACHEL'S DEATH AND BENJAMIN'S BIRTH

The story of Jacob continues with the death of his precious
wife Rachel. As they were traveling, Rachel went into labor and

died due to the difficult childbirth. And as she breathed her last, she named the son *Ben-Oni*, or "Son of My Sorrow." But his father called him "Son of My Right Hand," or Benjamin. Rachel had once passionately said to her husband, "Give me sons, or I'll die." And now that she had her children, she died. But by naming him "son of my sorrow," she left a legacy for him that Israel was not comfortable with. So he changed his name to "son of my right hand," or *Benjamin*. In giving his son that name, Jacob prophesied that the blessing would move on to the next generation.

We know that Rachel must have grieved knowing that she would never be able to raise her two boys. And so the phrase "Rachel is weeping" can be found in Matthew 2:16–18 and is used to describe the sorrow of Rachel weeping over sons she will never raise—the sons who would be killed by Herod seventeen hundred years later. Her tears were a prophecy of what was coming to her sons from the tribe of Benjamin who had settled near Bethlehem.

In the entire universe there is only one son that is both son of sorrow and son of the right hand. Jesus is his name! Christ has both of these two aspects to his name. Isaiah 53:3 describes him as "a man of deep sorrows" while Acts 2:33 tells us that "God exalted him to his right hand." There is no doubt that Benjamin was a type of the suffering and exalted Christ.

Jacob buried his beloved Rachel near the place where she died. And soon after his divine encounter at Bethel, he experienced one of the greatest sorrows of his heart. Great afflictions can follow great joys. Jacob sets up a pillar[34] over the tomb of Rachel at Bethlehem (1 Samuel 10:2), and Moses later stated that "to this day that pillar marks Rachel's tomb." While this may mean little to us, it mean so much to the Israelites as they came into the promised land centuries later under Joshua's leadership and saw Jacob's pillar. What a sense of history this pillar gave them.

I'm sure that Jacob felt like a drink offering being poured out to God at the death of Rachel. She was his dearest and closest. All of this happened close to Ephrath, which means "fruitful." On the way to the place called fruitfulness, God truly changed his servant Jacob. He was a man transformed by the visitation of God and the pain of sorrow. God's deep work had been accomplished in the "heel-grabber." Rachel died, but Israel journeyed on. And many, many years later, a son of Benjamin, named Paul, the apostle, would lead many into the ways of Christ (Philippians 3:5) in his journey to the nations.

THE DEATH OF ISAAC AT HEBRON

> Jacob came home to his father Isaac in Mamre, near Kiriath Arba (that is, Hebron), where Abraham and Isaac had lived as foreigners. Isaac was one hundred and eighty when he breathed his last and died. He died an old man and had lived a full life when he joined his ancestors. And his sons Esau and Jacob buried him there. (Genesis 35:27–29)

Israel, at last, came to Hebron. This was the home of his father Isaac and where his grandfather Abraham once dwelt. Israel made it home for the homegoing of his father. This was an emotional time for Jacob, losing his wife and his father. The age and death of Isaac was recorded, and by calculation, he lived the longest of all the patriarchs, one hundred and eighty years.

Isaac's death brought great wealth and blessing to Jacob. As the head of the family and heir of the covenant blessings, Jacob felt satisfied as he lived there in Hebron with the inheritance and blessings passed on from Isaac. He was about one hundred and twenty years old when Isaac died. And finally Jacob entered into full fellowship with God. (*Hebron* means "fellowship.") It's in this place of fellowship that we enjoy peace, satisfaction, and intimacy with God and others. Each of us must pass through Shechem (strength) and Bethel (the house of God) to Hebron (fellowship). Hebron signifies the place of maturity and fullness. For it was at Hebron that Jacob entered into full rest. Jacob was free at last to enjoy God in the place of sweet fellowship with his friend, his God.

So you have begun to set your eyes on the One who made Abraham a father of many nations. He is the covenant-keeper who will never disappoint you. He will do what he says he will do. And in the middle of your desert with nothing left, lay your head on the rock, the altar stone, and close your eyes. As the sands fade away and a ladder appears before you from out of heaven, go up and bring down all that is waiting for you there. As we discover God in all of his wonderful ways, we become his living altars. And as we completely offer up our lives to him, we become like our father Abraham, erecting our own altars throughout our desert journeys. Like Abraham, Isaac, and Jacob, we are to pass a generational blessing to our children. Is there one today that you could bless? With loving prayer, you can bless others around you today. Unite the generations with your blessing, and you will change the world!

LET'S PRAY

> God, I want to live each day in the blessing of heaven. You have filled me and satisfied me in your presence. All I desire is to be pleasing to you. I want to live in the fullness of my spiritual inheritance and in the fullness of your blessing on my life. You are a kind Father, a wonderful guide, and a strong tower for me. I love you, God. Amen.

ENDNOTES

1   The word *inheritance* is the Hebrew word *nachalah*, taken from the root word *nachal*, a homonym for "a flowing stream." An inheritance is the wealth of the father flowing down to the next generation.

2   Genesis 12:1. The Hebrew word *eretz* is etymologically linked to the Canaanite word *ratzon*, which means "firmness of will, stubbornness." God is saying to Abram with double meaning, "Leave your country but also leave your own will behind in order to enter God's plan." We need to leave it all behind, including our ideas of how God will work.

3   Genesis 12:2 can also be rendered "I will make your name great," which in the ancient Near East also implies being highly esteemed for his character. Also, the building of the tower of Babel was so that men could "make a name" for themselves. This was intended to be the gift of God and not something men could seize for themselves.

4   Genesis 12:3, which could also be translated "And by you all the families of the earth will bless themselves" or "Every nation will long for me to bless them as I have blessed you" (see Numbers 24:9; Isaiah 49:6; Galatians 3:8).

5   See Galatians 3:7–14.

6   *Shechem* means "shoulder," "the place of strength." Shechem

was the place where years later our Lord Jesus sat at the well of Jacob weary in his journey.

7   The great tree of Moreh was where God taught Abram to walk in faith not by sight. *Moreh* means "instruction." True spiritual knowledge comes from the strength of Christ. God will lead us to a place of true strength and instruct our heart to trust in him alone.

8   Paul, the Abraham of the New Testament, was a tentmaker.

9   Salem later became the city of Jeru*salem*.

10   In John 8:56, Jesus said that "Abraham rejoiced at the thought of seeing my day; he saw it and was glad." Abraham saw the day of Jesus as Melchizedek (a type of Jesus) came out to meet him with bread and wine, the elements of Holy Communion.

11   David, Solomon, and Hezekiah were kings and leaders who came from Abraham's blessed relationship with God, and that includes us. Yes, you and I are kings too! We have come into our kingship through the covenant God made with Abraham.

12   Genesis 17:8, where "descendants" could also be translated as "seed."

13   Perhaps the other two visitors were angels. Those who are careful to entertain strangers may be welcoming angels unawares (Hebrews 13:2).

14   Abraham also prepared the fatted calf, which is what the father in Luke 15 gave to his prodigal son when he returned in repentance.

15   See Leviticus 1 and 2 where the prescribed offerings are the very things Abraham and Sarah served their guests. These sacrifices in Leviticus were ordered 560 years after the time of Abraham.

16   To receive a covenant is not only receiving a new responsibility but also an obligation to release its power to multiple generations to come.

17   Six is the number of man. What would have happened if Abraham had asked the seventh time? But Abraham stopped at six times and ten people.

18   See Psalm 1.

19   *Zoar* means "small." An escape mentality will make us run from the mess but will take us to a small box where our dreams die and we protect our turf. The path of escapism is a path to "Smallville"—the place of self-preservation.

20   The name Yitzhak is the word *laughter* but in a form similar to the past tense. It could be translated "delayed laughter."

21   The word for mocking is *metzahek*, which is actually a form of *yitzahek* (Isaac). *Metzahek* means "laughter now," and *yitzahek* means "laughter delayed."

22   In Galatians 3–5, Paul interprets the narrative as the struggle with flesh and the Spirit. The flesh will always trust in works (the law), and the Spirit is always released by faith. Hagar represents the bondage of Sinai, Sarah the freedom of the promise. Once the promise is fulfilled, the old order must be done away with (driving out Hagar and Ishmael). Ishmael cannot become the heir.

23   See 1 Samuel 15:22.

24   The Hebrew word for *virgin, b'toolah,* means "a city." The virgin-bride of Christ is like a city—the New Jerusalem (Song of Songs 6:4; Revelation 21:2).

25   See Exodus 20:6.

26   See Genesis 25:11; 26:18–25.

27   *Beersheba* means "seven wells, complete, fulfillment, oath, covenant."

28   See Job 12:16.

29   Is this Isaiah's ascending "highway"? See Isaiah 35:8–9; 57:14–15; 62:10.

30   St. Germanus of Constantinople, *On the Divine Liturgy,* trans. Paul Meyendorff (Crestwood, NY: St Vladimir's Seminary Press, 1984), 101.

31   Leah's son Levi and his descendants became the priestly tribe of Israel.

32   *Gad* also means "a troop comes" (that is, many would follow after this one, an army fully prepared). The Lord has always had a troop in his heart, and a troop comes as the image of Jesus appears within his bride.

33   See Exodus 29:40–41; Numbers 6:17; 15:1–5; 28:7–10; 2 Samuel 23:16.

34   Jacob built two pillars in Genesis 35—one to his joy and one to his sorrow.

ABOUT THE AUTHORS

DR. BRIAN & CANDICE SIMMONS have been described as true pioneers in ministry. Their teaching and spiritual gifts have opened doors into several nations to bring the message of authentic awakening and revival to many. For many years, they have labored together to present Christ in his fullness wherever God sends them.

After a dramatic conversion to Christ in 1971, Brian and Candice answered the call of God to leave everything behind and become missionaries to unreached peoples. Taking their three children to the tropical rain forest of Central America, they planted churches for many years with the Paya-Kuna people group.

After their ministry overseas, Brian and Candice returned to North America, where they planted numerous ministries, including a dynamic church in New England (U.S.). They also established Passion & Fire Ministries, under which they travel full time as Bible teachers in service of local churches throughout the world.

Brian and Candice are co-authors of numerous books, Bible studies, and devotionals that help readers encounter God's heart and experience a deeper revelation of God as our Bridegroom

King, including *The Blessing, The Image Maker, The Sacred Journey, The Wilderness,* and *Throne Room Prayer.*

Dr. Simmons is also the lead translator of The Passion Translation®. The Passion Translation (TPT) is a heart-level translation that uses Hebrew, Greek, and Aramaic manuscripts to express God's fiery heart of love to this generation, merging the emotion and life-changing truth of God's Word.

Brian and Candice have been married since 1971 and have three children as well as precious grandchildren and great-grandchildren. Their passion is to live as loving examples of a spiritual father and mother to this generation.